D0952410

James Dickey

Twayne's United States Authors Series

Warren French, Editor
Indiana University, Indianapolis

TUSAS 451

JAMES DICKEY
(1923–   )
Photograph by Mark Morrow

James Dickey

By Richard J. Calhoun
and Robert W. Hill

Clemson University

Twayne Publishers • *Boston*

James Dickey

Richard J. Calhoun
Robert W. Hill

Copyright © 1983 by G.K. Hall & Company
All Rights Reserved
Published by Twayne Publishers
A Division of G. K. Hall & Company
70 Lincoln Street
Boston, Massachusetts 02111

Book Production by Marne B. Sultz

Book Design by Barbara Anderson

Printed on permanent/durable acid-free
paper and bound in the United States of
America.

**Library of Congress Cataloging in
Publication Data**

Calhoun, Richard James.
James Dickey.

(Twayne's United States authors series ;
TUSAS 451)
Bibliography: p. 145
Includes index.
1. Dickey, James—Criticism and interpretation.
I. Hill, Robert W., 1941–   .
II. Title.   III. Series.
PS3554.I32Z59   1983   811'.54   83-4380
ISBN 0-8057-7391-6

For Doris, who puts up with Dick,
and Jane, who understands Bob and all the rest of this

Contents

About the Authors

Richard J. Calhoun is Alumni Professor of English at Clemson University. He received the Ph.D. from the University of North Carolina in 1959. He is editor of *James Dickey: The Expansive Imagination*, published by Everett/Edwards, Inc., in 1973. He is coeditor with John C. Guilds of *The Tricentennial Anthology of South Carolina*, published by the University of South Carolina Press in 1971, and, with Ernest M. Lander, Jr., coeditor of *Two Decades of Change: The South Since the Supreme Court Desegregation Decision*, published by the University of South Carolina Press in 1975. He has been editor and coeditor of the *South Carolina Review* since 1973. He has published articles on contemporary poets and contemporary literary criticism and on southern literature in *Southern Literary Journal, Mississippi Quarterly, South Atlantic Bulletin, South Carolina Review*, and *Southern Review*. He edited a series of cassette tapes on contemporary American poets for Everett/Edwards. Professor Calhoun has held Fulbright lectureships in American literature in Yugoslavia and in Denmark.

Robert W. Hill is Associate Professor of English and Director of English Graduate Studies at Clemson University. He received the Ph.D. from the University of Illinois in 1972. He has been coeditor of the *South Carolina Review* since 1973. He has published articles on Yeats, Hopkins, Frost, Roethke, Nemerov, and Dickey; his poems have appeared in *Ascent, Southern Review, Southern Poetry Review*, and *Shenandoah*, and his fiction in the *Davidson Miscellany*. He also edits *Billy Goat*. From 1972 to 1978 he wrote and hosted "Poetry Today," a weekly program on the South Carolina Educational Radio Network.

Preface

During James Dickey's days when he was engaged in what he described as "barnstorming for poetry"—actually reading his poems for a small fee at colleges and universities on a poetry circuit—the authors of this volume were his hosts at Clemson University. We asked the coordinator of the poetry circuit to which Clemson had attached itself: "How shall we know him?" We were told, "You can't miss him. He'll be the biggest guy getting off the plane, and he'll be carrying the biggest guitar." All this was true.

He also brought along his new book, *Buckdancer's Choice,* for which he had just won the National Book Award, and a selection of his other books of poetry. No collected edition of his poems had been published then. The time was 1966, and for Dickey, coming to Clemson to read was something of a homecoming. He had begun college here in 1942, played freshman football with some distinction, studied very little, and departed soon after the end of the football season for the Army Air Force. All of this Dickey remembered. His memory for details was phenomenal. He asked about teachers he had had twenty-four years before at Clemson; and he remembered names, physical appearance, and personality traits. He had been far from a poet then, but he noticed things about people. Though his career at Clemson was brief, there had been something memorable about him even then, for his former teachers without exception remembered him.

His reading that night was the best by a poet within the memory of anyone present, but then there had not been a great many poets reading at Clemson. More followed on his heels because students wanted to see whether there were any other poets like James Dickey. His readings of poems like "Cherrylog Road" and "The Bee" (dedicated to Clemson football coaches) established the kind of connection between poet and audience that Dickey desires between persona and reader in his poems. Dickey wants to compel belief from his readers, and that night his listeners believed him absolutely, even though much of what he read was what Dickey has described in his criticism as "creative lies." The reading was not without controversy. His reading of "The Sheep Child," together with his introductory comments, created a generation gap of conflicting responses among his audience. The students responded with enthusiasm; a few of the adults voiced complaints.

A recollection of this incident is appropriate to introduce a book on James Dickey, for it was James Dickey, the reader of his poetry on the road, who created an audience of readers for that poetry. Those who had heard him could hear his voice and experience some of this personality in the poems, appropriately because one of Dickey's aims has been to restore the poet to the poem. The readings also helped to create the legends, something missing from poetry readings since Dylan Thomas had read his poetry at American college campuses. Dickey's appearance on campuses had become by the late 1960s a major event. By the end of the decade, with the publication of *Poems 1957–1967,* James Dickey had become a major poet, called by a Boston critic, no less, the nearest rival to Robert Lowell. This was a remarkable achievement for a poet who had been writing seriously for only one decade, beginning late with the publication of his first book when he was thirty-seven.

In the 1980s Dickey is still a major poet, and the author of a significant novel and three volumes of reviews and criticism. His novel, *Deliverance,* is a contemporary classic with something of a cultish following among white-water adventurers, cliff climbers, and survivalists. College students respond to it today even more enthusiastically than they did in the 1970s. He may not have enhanced his reputation as a poet in the 1970s, but he has now published a dozen volumes of poetry, demonstrating a great range in themes and in poetic forms. Dickey is an experimenter, whether in something as simple as returning to simple declarative sentences or as complex as the hallucinating stream-of-consciousness of *The Zodiac.* His importance to postmodernism as poet and critic has not been fully appreciated. After all, Dickey wrote reviews at a time of great change in poetry for a significant literary periodical, the *Sewanee Review.*

Dickey's opposition to certain new movements, like the Beats and "confessional" poetry, is well known. But his commitment to open forms and his determined resistance to T. S. Eliot's dictum that modern poetry should be impersonal are among his contributions to a postmodernist aesthetics that have been virtually ignored. James Dickey as poet, novelist, and critic has been too glibly regarded as a conservative without significant social meaning. Robert Bly's attack on him for apparently not supporting protest by writers against the war in Vietnam left its mark on subsequent Dickey commentaries. Or he has been regarded as a romantic proponent of the "more life" school. One New York poet, reading in

Scandinavia, summed up his case against Dickey both inaccurately and ineloquently: "James Dickey—he is just a Southern redneck."

This introduction to James Dickey as poet, novelist, and critic attempts to show that the man is anything but simple, that his activities have been diverse, and that his poetic voices represent many selves. In the 1960s and 1970s Dickey's reputation as reader and lecturer was legendary and often salacious; but that public posture is just one aspect of Dickey's solid career as writer, university professor, and businessman. Although the best way to evaluate Dickey's work is to begin with the poetry, he should be regarded as a whole literary figure, a prolific writer in many genres, whose accomplishments are of one variegated piece.

Clemson University   Richard J. Calhoun
                                                             Robert W. Hill

Acknowledgments

From *Babel to Byzantium* by James Dickey. © 1968 by James Dickey. Reprinted by permission of Farrar, Straus & Giroux, Inc.

From *Deliverance* by James Dickey. © 1970 by James Dickey. Reprinted by permission of Houghton Mifflin Co.

From *Drowning with Others* by James Dickey. © 1962 by James Dickey. Reprinted by permission of Wesleyan University Press.

From *The Eye-Beaters, Blood, Victory, Madness, Buckhead and Mercy* by James Dickey. © 1970 by James Dickey. Reprinted by permission of Doubleday & Co., Inc.

From *God's Images: The Bible, a New Vision* by James Dickey. © 1977 by Oxmoor House, Inc. Reprinted by permission of the publisher.

From *Into the Stone* by James Dickey, in *Poets of Today VII* edited by John Hall Wheelock. © 1960. Reprinted by permission of Charles Scribner's and Sons, Inc.

From *Jericho: The South Beheld* by James Dickey. © 1974 by Oxmoor House, Inc. Reprinted by permission of the publisher.

From *Poems 1957–1967* by James Dickey. © 1967 by James Dickey. Reprinted by permission of Wesleyan University Press.

From *Puella* by James Dickey. © 1982 by James Dickey. Reprinted by permission of Doubleday & Co., Inc.

From *Self-Interviews* by James Dickey. © 1970 by James Dickey. Reprinted by permission of Doubleday & Co., Inc.

From *Sorties* by James Dickey. © 1971 by James Dickey. Reprinted by permission of Doubleday & Co., Inc.

From *The Strength of Fields* by James Dickey. © 1979 by James Dickey. Reprinted by permission of Doubleday & Co., Inc.

From *The Zodiac* by James Dickey. © 1976 by James Dickey. Reprinted by permission of Doubleday & Co., Inc.

Abbreviations

Throughout the text, the following abbreviations are used to identify page references to these works by James Dickey. See the Selected Bibliography for identification of editions:

BB	*Babel to Byzantium*
BC	*Buckdancer's Choice*
D	*Deliverance*
DWO	*Drowning with Others*
EB	*The Eye-Beaters . . .*
GI	*God's Images*
H	*Helmets*
IS	*Into the Stone and Other Poems*
J	*Jericho*
P	*Poems 1957–1967*
S	*Sorties*
SF	*The Strength of Fields*
SI	*Self-Interviews*
SP	*The Suspect in Poetry*
Z	*The Zodiac*

Chronology

1923   James Lafayette Dickey born 2 February, Atlanta, Georgia. Father, Eugene Dickey, an Atlanta lawyer. Mother, Maibelle Swift Dickey. Older brother, Eugene, died four years before James was born.

1942   Graduated from North Fulton High School, where he starred in football. Attended Clemson A&M College, played football there, and left before the end of the first semester to join the Army Air Force.

1942–1946   Flew approximately 100 missions for 418th Night Fighters in South Pacific. Participated in firebombings of major Japanese cities.

1948   Married Maxine Syerson, 4 November, in Rossville, Georgia.

1949   A.B. degree from Vanderbilt University.

1950   M.A. degree from Vanderbilt University—thesis topic: "Symbol and Imagery in the Shorter Poems of Herman Melville." Taught at Rice Institute in Houston, Texas, September to Christmastime, then recalled by Air Force for service in Korean War.

1951   Christopher Swift born 31 August.

1952–1954   Returned to teach at Rice Institute. *Sewanee Review* Fellowship. Lived, traveled, wrote in Europe.

1955–1956   Taught at University of Florida. Resigned after complaints about a poem he read at public reading. Began career in advertising as copywriter for McCann–Erickson in New York City. Worked next three years with other advertising firms in New York and Atlanta.

1958   Union League Civic and Arts Foundation Prize (*Poetry: A Magazine of Verse*). Kevin Webster born 18 August.

1959   Vachel Lindsay Prize. Longview Foundation Award.

1960   *Into the Stone.*

1961   Guggenheim Fellowship awarded.

1962   Traveled in Europe and wrote during 1962–63. Home base, Positina, Italy. *Drowning with Others.*

1963   Poet-in-Residence at Reed College, 1963–64.

1964   Poet-in-Residence at San Fernando Valley State College, 1964–65. *Two Poems of the Air. The Suspect in Poetry. Helmets.*

1965   *Buckdancer's Choice.*

1966   National Book Award for *Buckdancer's Choice.* Melville Cane Award (Poetry Society of America). National Institute of Arts and Letters Award. Poet-in-Residence at University of Wisconsin, Madison. Appointed Consultant in Poetry for the Library of Congress, 1966–68.

1967   *Poems 1957–1967.*

1968   *Babel to Byzantium.*

1969   Appointed Carolina Professor of English and Writer-in-Residence at University of South Carolina.

1970   *Deliverance. The Eye–Beaters, Blood, Victory, Madness, Buckhead and Mercy. Self–Interviews.*

1971   *Sorties.* Prix Medicis. *New York Quarterly* Poetry Day Award.

1972   Script writer and consultant for movie version of *Deliverance.* Acted part of sheriff in movie.

1974   *Jericho: The South Beheld.*

1975   Script writer for television production of *The Call of the Wild.*

1976   Wife, Maxine Syerson, died, 28 October. *The Zodiac.* "Cahill Is Blind" in *Esquire.* Married Deborah Dodson, 30 December.

1977   *God's Images.* Read his poem "The Strength of Fields" at inaugural celebration for Jimmy Carter.

1978   *Tucky the Hunter. In Pursuit of the Grey Soul. The Enemy from Eden.*

1979   *The Strength of Fields.*

1980   *The Water Bug's Mittens* (the 1979 Ezra Pound Lecture, University of Idaho).

1981   Daughter, Bronwen, born 16 May, in Columbia, S.C. Five poems from *Puella,* published in *Poetry: A Magazine of Verse,* win Levinson Prize.

1982   *Puella,* 11 June. Multi–media presentation based on *Puella,* at Arizona State University, 14 May. *Värmland: Poems Based on Poems.*

Chapter One

James Dickey:
A Biographical Sketch

The Many Selves of James Dickey

Few contemporary writers have told more about what they wanted to tell about themselves than James Dickey. He is no doubt the most interviewed and self-interviewed poet of his time, and he has told more about the origins and composition of his literary works than almost any American writer since Henry James. His life has been varied, and that versatility is central to an understanding of his works. What he has said about the role of the self in poetry—that there should be many different selves in the poet—has been true of his life as well. Some critics have focused too narrowly on one Dickey, especially on the physical and visceral Dickey, while ignoring the others. There is the creative artist—as evidenced by Dickey the poet, the novelist, the critic, the screenwriter and TV writer, the frequently interviewed poet. But there is another self that he has consciously promoted—the guitarist, the hunter with bow and arrow, the macho writer, the considerably over-thirty poet whose poetry readings nevertheless established rapport with under-thirty audiences beyond that of any American poet since the Beats. There is also the more provincial Dickey, the southern poet who could be almost perfectly cast in the movie version of his own novel *Deliverance* as a backwoods southern sheriff.

The Dickey private self most often overlooked is a more cosmopolitan and sophisticated James Dickey—the successful advertising director in New York City and Atlanta, the honor graduate from Vanderbilt, the university professor at South Carolina, the translator-imitator of contemporary Russian poetry,[1] the friend of Yevtushenko but also of William Buckley, and the lover of Italy, and even the book collector. This Dickey is clearly an intellectual who has taken care to disguise his learning.

1

What all this signifies is that Dickey has not only desired to open up to his readers a much greater accessibility to experience but has also sought to maintain this accessibility in his own life. This does not mean that Dickey is a nineteenth-century "cult of experience writer" who must live all he writes but one who believes that he must be able to see the potential within himself for what he can imagine as happenings in his poetry and in his fiction.

There are some areas of his personal experience that he has written little or nothing about. He has written about family, war, hunting, sports, and middle age, but very little about his life as a university professor, or even candidly about how his desire for accessibility to experience led to occasional nearly Rabelaisian experiences that made him something of a legend in his own time on the poetry circuits. He has indicated in recent interviews how his life-style has changed, how he once thought alcohol was an aid to creativity but now realizes that for an aging poet it can also be a disaster.[2] Dickey is, after all, a positive poet, a survivor of the destruction of war who wants to be a celebrator of life. Consequently, in his use of material from his own life he is much more a positive than a negative romantic.

The Early Years

James Dickey's roots are in the South, but not the agrarian South. He was born and reared in the urban South of Atlanta, Georgia. He was the second child of an Atlanta lawyer, Eugene Dickey, and his wife, Maibelle. Their first child, Eugene, died four years before James was born, a family tragedy that fascinated Dickey as a child.

His father encouraged him to read, but in law rather than literature. Dickey recalls that either his father read to him records of famous cases "from the trial of Jesus Christ up to the trial of Fatty Arbuckle," the great movie comic of the 1920s, or they read famous cases to each other (*SI*, 26). He makes it clear that great lawyers, not great poets, were the heroes in his family. A special hero to his father was Clarence Darrow, and the favorite dramas of father and son were the real-life Clarence Darrow–William Jennings Bryan encounter in the Scopes "monkey trial" of 1924 or Sargent Prentice's eloquent defense of "some Mississippi boys on trial for murder in Tennessee" (*SI*, 26). His mother would occasionally quote from Longfellow or from Tennyson, but Dickey's own early appreciation of literature was pretty much limited to an admiration for Lord Byron that followed his reading John Drinkwater's biography *The Pilgrim of Eternity*.

Dickey's main interests as a boy were in carpentry and in athletics, especially football. He played well enough at North Fulton High School in Atlanta to attend, after graduation, Clemson College, 125 miles away in South Carolina, in order to play at a school that was rapidly becoming a sports power. He entered Clemson in the fall of 1942 and played for the freshman team, achieving special distinction for his determined running as a wingback in the freshman game against Clemson's main rival, the University of South Carolina.[3]

The certainty of being drafted into military service in World War II, and the time devoted to football, distracted him from his studies so much that when he left Clemson to enlist in the Army Air Force soon after the conclusion of the football season, he was passing only one course—freshman English. When he returned to Clemson to read his poetry in 1966, his English teacher, Claud Green, remarked that of all the students he had had, he would have thought James Dickey one of the least likely to become a poet.

Dickey's first extensive reading of poetry began in the Air Force, or as he likes to tell college audiences, while waiting among the books for a post librarian he was dating to get off duty. Dickey was in the Air Force from 1942 to 1946, heavily involved in combat, flying nearly one hundred combat missions for the 418th Night Fighters in the Pacific campaign in the Philippines, at Okinawa, and participating in the firebombing of major Japanese cities.

His reading of poetry in the post libraries continued. His desire to be a writer came, however, more from reading "failed poets" who turned to narrative fiction and to prose. Dickey recounts that after a typhoon in Okinawa "there were books scattered all over the place—and I read whatever I laid hands on. Novels. Prose. But I sensed immediately that writers like Faulkner or Wolfe had a different orientation with language than, say, Maugham. I responded to this quality. I kept looking for writers who had this thing. Melville. James Agee. I felt writers like this were sort of failed poets who were trying to use prose for higher things; if those fellows were aspiring for something higher, I thought that was the direction to go."[4]

After his discharge Dickey changed from Clemson College to Vanderbilt University and from football to track, becoming the Tennessee state champion in the 120-yard high hurdles. He was cognizant of entering as a twenty-three-year-old freshman a university with a strong recent literary tradition developed by Allen Tate, Robert Penn Warren, Cleanth Brooks, and Donald Davidson, who had fostered the Fugitive movement in the

1920s, Agrarianism in the 1930s, and the New Criticism in the 1940s. Dickey has never regarded himself as a "latter-day Agrarian"; but he "read around a good deal in the works" of the Vanderbilt writers, and he has always shared some of their critical misgivings about urbanization, industrialization, and logical positivism (*SI,* 34). As an English major at Vanderbilt he also read the then-controversial New Criticism—the Brooks and Warren formalist stress on the language used by poets and on the dramatic nature of poetry. This literary tradition at Vanderbilt and the presence still there of men like Donald Davidson and historian Frank Owsley made him aware of "what it really meant for me to be a Southerner" (*SI,* 35). The former Vanderbilt writers who appealed to Dickey most strongly were Robert Penn Warren for the violence in his works and Randall Jarrell for the "humanistic feeling of compassion and gentleness about him" (*SI,* 34).

Three teachers at Vanderbilt had a direct influence on Dickey. The first was his freshman English instructor, William Hunter, who praised his first composition, an essay on the invasion of Okinawa, and who permitted him to write on any topic he chose. Dickey obliged by turning out critical articles, poems, even a surrealistic play, building up his confidence in his writing abilities. The second teacher was Monroe Spears, who impressed Dickey that a fine critical mind could devote itself to literature rather than to science or engineering. Spears, later a distinguished critic of contemporary literature but at that time primarily an eighteenth-century scholar, got his pupil interested in neoclassical poetry and stressed the importance of "measure, form, and wit" (*SI,* 30–31). Dickey even credits Spears with helping him as a poet to escape literalism in poetry through getting him to see "the creative possibilities of the lie" and to become less contrained by fact, the way things had actually happened. The third influential teacher was Carl Siefert, an astronomer who conveyed to Dickey his own sense of reassurance in the face of chaos by finding universal laws operating in the universe. Dickey also became interested in anthropology, especially in primitive tribes and in the difference between their outlook and that of so-called civilized people. This interest of the student then clearly became a concern of the poet later.

On 4 November 1948, James Dickey married Maxine Syerson in a ceremony held above a feed store in Rossville, Georgia (*SI,* 39). The following June he graduated from Vanderbilt *magna cum laude,* and he was awarded a graduate fellowship in English more on the basis of his grades and of several critical papers he had written than as the result of his fledgling promise as a poet with one poem published in the student literary magazine and another accepted by the prestigious *Sewanee Review.* Dickey completed the M.A. in English in 1950 and accepted a teaching position at Rice University in Houston, Texas. But the need for pilots at the outbreak of the Korean War led to his recall by the Air Force.

When Dickey returned to teaching at Rice in 1952 after his second stint in the Air Force, he was past thirty and not yet well begun on a career. Without a Ph.D. and working under a department head who insisted on the doctorate for tenure, Dickey turned seriously to writing poetry. His old mentor at Vanderbilt, Monroe Spears, now at Rice, suggested that he apply for a *Sewanee Review* fellowship. The poems Dickey submitted were judged by old Vanderbiltians Andrew Lytle and Allen Tate, and the award was granted. He took his family to Europe in 1954 and wrote more poems, even having a few accepted for publication. After a stay in Europe, he was asked by Andrew Lytle to join him at the University of Florida, in 1955, where Lytle was teaching creative writing. Disappointingly, Dickey's responsibilities were mostly teaching freshman composition rather than creative writing at a time when he had decided that his career might very well be in poetry. The appointment terminated whatever residual plans he had left for an academic career, for when Dickey read a poem called "The Father's Body," intended to express his sensual experience of a child recognizing the physical differences between himself and his father, the audience, mostly faculty wives and ladies of Gainesville, was shocked.[5] When an apology was demanded, Dickey refused, resigning instead. He had taken the first of two major risks that would actually further his development as a poet.

Advertising by Day, Poetry by Night

In April 1956 at the age of thirty-three Dickey began a new career as copywriter with the New York advertising firm of McCann-Erickson with primary responsibility for the Coca-Cola account. He had not resigned his other career as a poet, writing advertising copy by day and poetry by night, publishing in numerous little magazines and even a few poems in large magazines like the *Hudson Review,* and making friends with and receiving encouragement from other writers. His poetry was rapidly becoming more important to him as the writing he really wanted to do than was the advertising he was being paid to do. In 1958 Dickey returned home to Atlanta continuing to specialize on the Coca-Cola account but

writing more and more poetry. Dickey relates an incident that illustrates
the differences between the world of advertising copy and that of writing
poetry:

> I wrote this poem "The Heaven of Animals" in an advertising office. I had a
> new secretary and I asked her to type it for me. She typed up the poem
> letter-perfect and brought it to me. Then she asked, "What is it? What
> company does it go to?"
> "This is a poem," I said.
> "It is?"
> "Yes, it is, I hope."
> "What are we going to sell with it?" she asked.
> "God," I said. "We're going to sell God."
> "Does this go to a religious magazine or something?"
> "No, I'm going to publish it in the *New Yorker*," I told her. And, as it
> happened, that's where it came out. (*SI,* 108)

When his business still interfered with the increasing time demanded
by his poetry, he sacrificed once more by changing jobs to a smaller
advertising firm, Liller Neal, where he worked on advertising for other
Atlanta-based firms like Lay's Potato Chips. Finally, he took a position as
creative director and vice-president of another Atlanta agency, Burke
Dowling Adams, which handled the Delta Airlines account. He had also
secured more time to write poetry and to plan his first volume (*SI,* 45).

"Barnstorming for Poetry"

Very shortly he had enough poems to publish two books, *Into the Stone* in
1960 and *Drowning with Others* in 1962. His successful publishing debut
and a Guggenheim Fellowship, combined with a belief that there was
something wrong about saying "things that people pay you to say," led to
his final break with the business world (*SI,* 44). Dickey went to Europe for
nine months, with Italy as his main base of operations, and worked hard on
a third book of poems, *Helmets*.

On his return to America he served the next four years as a poet-in-
residence—first at Reed College in Oregon (1963–64), then at San
Fernando Valley State College in California (1964–65), and at last at the
University of Wisconsin, Madison (1966). *Helmets* appeared in 1964, and
Buckdancer's Choice (1965) brought Dickey his first major recognition, the
National Book Award in 1966. During this time Dickey was often on the

road reading his poetry at various campuses across the country, as described in his essay "Barnstorming for Poetry" (*BB*, 249–57). Dickey received the most prestigious appointment the federal government offers a poet when he was named Consultant in Poetry for the Library of Congress in 1966. During his two-year term he gave the customary number of lectures and sponsored for the Library Archives an uncustomary number of lectures and recordings by writers like John Updike, John Cheever, and William Stafford, reading from their own works. In 1967, the publication of *Poems 1957–1967* made possible a view of just how remarkable his achievements during a decade of writing poetry had been. In 1969, Dickey accepted the appointment he still holds as Carolina Professor of English and Writer-in-Residence at the University of South Carolina in Columbia.

In the 1970s, Dickey's production of poetry waned, and his interest in prose increased. After the popular success of *Deliverance,* a second novel was planned, entitled at various times *Death's Baby Machine, Alnilam,* and *A Minor Constellation,* a work still in progress. He combined interviews with critical essays to produce *Self-Interviews* in 1970 and *Sorties* in 1971. More than a dozen other interviews were published elsewhere. A new interest, movie and television script-writing, developed as a result of Dickey's involvement in the motion-picture production of *Deliverance.* When studio casting failed to deliver a satisfactory southern sheriff, Dickey was cast in the role himself. In 1975 he created for television a version of Jack London's *The Call of the Wild.* One of his greatest popular—and financial—triumphs was a literary work for the coffee-table, *Jericho: The South Beheld* (1974), descriptions of southern landscapes to accompany drawings and paintings by Hubert Shuptrine. *Jericho* was followed in 1977 by a second, less extravagantly successful prose poem, *God's Images,* with etchings by Marvin Hayes. Truthfully to describe the consensus of literary critics and reviewers would be to say that surely the quantity and probably the quality of Dickey's poetry severely declined in the 1970s with the publication of *The Eye-Beaters, Blood, Victory, Madness, Buckhead and Mercy* in 1970, *The Zodiac* in 1976, and *The Strength of Fields* in 1979.

It is equally truthful, however, to say that we disagree in large measure with that consensus, which now has become the most facile kind of commentary on Dickey. The serious decline in quantity of poetry is undeniable. But, standing with Richard Howard, who calls *The Eye-Beaters* "giant utterance";[6] with Robert Penn Warren, who says of *The*

Zodiac, ". . . the audacity of imagery, assemblage of rhythms, the power of language redeems all—in a period too often marked by a delicate hovering over the fragile merely because it is fragile and the prosy because it is prosy, the celebration of sensibility as such, polite or academic scrupulosities, self-pity in a cruel world, craven free verse lacking basic and projective rhythms";[7] and with Dave Smith, who speaks of "the general and significant accomplishment of *The Strength of Fields*";[8] we find that the demands made upon his readers by the many-selved, expansive Dickey are too much for some of them to accept without displeasure. This is not to claim stupidly that all Dickey's later works are devoid of problems, even failures, but the continuity of the poet's career is both distinguishable and distinguished. Dickey continues to take not just the safe, familiar way in his poems but also the ways that stretch the limits of the art, the artist, and the audience. Unlike the eighty-seven-year-old Robert Frost, who read at the inauguration of John F. Kennedy and who had run out the string of his creative powers, Dickey, the poet of Jimmy Carter's inauguration, seems in his most recent work to be anticipating new efforts and new successes.

Chapter Two

Reaching Inward: A Thirty-Seven-Year-Old First-Book Poet

Dickey's first collection, "Into the Stone and Other Poems," was published by Scribner's in the three-in-one volume, *Poets of Today VII* (1960).[1] In the only book he ever labeled so baldly, Dickey separated these early poems into four groups—"Family," "War," "Death, and Others," and "Love." But these broad, unsurprising subjects also interweave complexly with the poet's unlabeled aggressive desire for nature's nonhuman (or primordial human) energy. Such urgency to acquire what might normally be called *super*natural powers leads this modern, suburban James Dickey to mystery and a concomitant need for fresh access to ritual.

Dickey's conviction that humankind has lost its natural force is reiterated in later works as diverse as "The Sheep Child" (1966), "Falling" (1967), "May Day Sermon" (1967), and *Deliverance* (1970). The loss is most grievous in terms of physical grace and spiritual excitement; the poet desires wholeness. Dickey's neo-romanticism includes a reverence for instinct and intuition, often requiring a person momentarily to put away reason, to withdraw from traditional social communion, to be alone to tap the sensual imagination. Even in so civilized an activity as poetry, rational modes must sometimes be prevented:

> . . . I turn the page
> Of the notebook, carefully not
>
> Remembering what I have written,
> For now . . .
> The poem is beginning to move. . . .
> ("A Dog Sleeping on My Feet," 1962)

9

These unnameable forces appear in terms of image and experience, but the poet's sincere conviction is reflected in such lines as "One *must* think of this" ("The Movement of Fish," 1961, our italics). An evangelist for modern romanticism, Dickey believes the aggressive pursuit is essential—truly of the essence of the human beast. To lose the "pine-prickling legs" that carry us to intuitive knowledge is to become shells of people, shadows of the true human glory.

Although none of his four declared topics even hints at this major theme, the title, "Into the Stone," does make it clear that some kind of imaginative interchange is possible between the human and the nonhuman worlds. For Dickey, nature is artistically and philosophically—even physically—essential for human beings to apprehend rightly. This early in his career (but at a relatively late age, thirty-seven), Dickey stakes out his major source of energy and knowledge—the natural world of palpable reality and immanent spirit. Fully half of the two dozen poems in this first volume are dominated by nature imagery (the five-poem "War" section is not), and the human speaker of each poem is characteristically drawn to new power and insight. Although these first poems are almost exclusively grounded in vegetative and inanimate, rather than animate, figures, the overlapping of themes and images produces the coherent "worldly mysticism" Laurence Lieberman recognized as central to Dickey's imaginative universe.[2] Nature, Dickey insists, can be haunted by a willfully seeking human being; its visions are available for persons to learn of life and death.

Ritual, Regeneration, and Ecstasy

"Sleeping Out at Easter," the opening poem of *Into the Stone,* depicts a man's personal regeneration ritual. What he seeks is found partly by his conscious attention to physical things around him. He sleeps out (not very spectacularly) in his own backyard, with his son asleep in the house and his wife at the window next morning—pointedly Easter—thus to enact the connection of all human creatures with the seasonal, vegetative world. As Dickey says in *Self-Interviews,* "His rebirth is symbolized by nothing more or less than waking up in a strange place which is near a familiar place" (*SI,* 86). But other things, from within, also contribute. Specifically, his education and his religious tradition are inextricably wound with his instincts and intuitions. His allusions to "Word" (Logos) and "king" are signs of resurrection; his graves and light, seeds and death, reverberate with overtones of Christian and pagan springtime.

Recognizing that to read a poem about ecstasy is as far from ecstasy as sleeping out is from Christly resurrection, Dickey nevertheless nudges his readers toward their subliminal apprehension of natural forces. In "The Poet Turns on Himself" (*BB,* 283 ff.), he explains that this was the first poem he wrote in which he felt his distinctive, compelling inner rhythms, the prearticulate impulse, perhaps, reported by Symboliste poets like Mallarmé and Verlaine, or critics like Jacques Maritain and Ezra Pound, who trace the making of word-art to natural body rhythms so far withdrawn from human consciousness that they are unrecognizable even when they surface, except to a few poets, musicians, and their best audiences. It is this edge-of-consciousness enlightenment that leads Dickey to write so often of sleep, dreams, and various altered states of mind. Especially in later works like "The Sheep Child," "Falling," *Deliverance,* and *The Zodiac,* these alterations are by extreme, even outrageous, circumstances. To relocate the point of view, to lead the reader to different perspectives, "carefully not / Remembering," is to allow a new remembering, almost a Wordsworthian retrieval of primal truths, veneered or blotted by civilized training.

Paradoxically, as Dickey strives for the dislocation of normal human consciousness, the goal being to achieve some more natural condition, he exercises a great deal of rational control. In trying to be natural, he runs into the same sort of problem D. H. Lawrence has in *trying* to be instinctually sexual. Dickey's ideal synthesis of the rational and the nonrational corresponds to what John Hall Wheelock describes as "personality,"[3] the unforced, emerging self that preexists any truly creative act. For Dickey, that ideal synthesis has inspired a career-long interest in formal experimentation.

Again, "Sleeping Out at Easter" is a touchstone. Two of its six stanzas are italicized, indicating a state of consciousness other than the immediate narrator's. An oracular, echoing voice uses the concluding lines of each stanza as refrains, accreting until the final stanza is constructed entirely of lines excerpted from the preceding stanzas. Such incantation charms readers into the narrator's own mystical communion. In this innovative form ("a kind of refrain technique that, so far as I know, I invented for the occasion," *BB,* 285), Dickey implies that everyone's spiritual lust is to find another voice—a true voice—within oneself; to escape from complacent, electrified houses; if only for a brief time to feel the light drawn out of all things, pulled with mysterious purpose by the trees into the forest.

"Sleeping Out at Easter" recounts an experience other poets might have tried to make into a lyric—fixed and timeless—but the anapestic narration works against freezing or abrogating time. Dickey wants to tell the process of mortal recovery from (lamentably) rare excursions into the world of the *natural spiritual*: "I . . . wanted to see if I could work with narrative elements in new and maybe peculiar ways. . . . I liked to make use of the element of time in a poem instead of having a conventional lyric approach in which a moment of perception, of extreme sensibility is presented" (*SI,* 135–36). His aesthetic preference for narration corroborates Dickey's belief in Heraclitean change and process as the essential human condition. He is also persuaded that the fixed and normal human mentality, the dulled and clouded, must be "energized,"[4] shaken apart, refocused, enlightened.

Consequently, he often chooses to obscure or drastically relocate sensory and intellectual bench-marks. "Sleeping Out at Easter" begins with the visual perspective of an animal. As with the seabird *qua homo sapiens* in "Reincarnation (II)" (1964), this narrator is seen initially as a nonhuman creature waking up, coming gradually to be aware of his own condition. In a sense, Dickey gives readers new eyes, and in so doing he may resort to bizarre images of sight. Not choosing the more abstract path of Emerson's fantasy ("I become a transparent eye-ball"), Dickey's sleeper says, "My animal eyes become human," claiming kinship with the natural world, charming the readers to acquiesce in his "magical shepherd's" spell. For Dickey, the making of poetry, like the simple beholding of the world, is a magical thing before which we all should be ashamed in our plodding pragmatism and our boorish, familiar ignorance. Bizarre as they may sometimes be, Dickey's poems heighten and illuminate real things, often rendering transcendent visions which return his readers to the world to see it as they never had before.

The Ritual of Family Connection

In delving "into the stone" (which stone is *us*), Dickey understands that to seek natural, cosmic connections one must pursue and confirm family connections. His first-volume "Family" poems encompass wife, sons, father, and mother, with "The Signs," "The Call," and "The Game" specifically about fathers protecting sons. But most striking of these figures is the spirit of a dead brother whom Dickey never knew in his life. Although he has consistently scorned the "confessional poets" and does not generally parade his private emotions, he had admitted guilt at being alive only because his parents' first son, Eugene, had died of spinal meningitis in 1919 at the age of six: ". . . I *did* gather by implication and hints of family relatives that my mother, an invalid with angina pectoris, would not have dared to have another child if Gene had lived. . . . And I have always felt a sense of guilt that my birth depended on my brother's death" (*SI*, 89). "The String" makes Dickey's brother-guilt explicit and echoes it with a mournful refrain: *"Dead before I was born."* The poem is rather stark in its opening lines, "Except when he enters my son, / The same age as he at his death, / I cannot bring my brother to myself." But, as Laurence Lieberman points out, "the dying brother's string-tricks such as 'foot of a crow,' are conceived of as the ritual magic act that can guarantee his eternal return in living beings."[5] The parents are not consoled by the ritual, but the narrator's consolation of the family ties through his own son, through his parents, and to his dead brother affirms the ritual act as love.

Several of Dickey's poems evoke the ghostly presence of the brother, who does not quite accuse, as Dickey's guilt might allow; but he does not comfort, either. It is perhaps this ambivalence that impels the poet toward adventures with other mystical presences, different, but owing something of their urgency to the family ghost who laid such unfair claims upon the younger James Dickey.

"The Underground Stream" combines the themes of nature and brother-guilt. The narrator accomplishes a claustrophobic sort of ecstasy, sinking through the earth to the stream which deep-feeds the well. In some ways, this poem recalls John Donne's "The Ecstasie," in which two lovers' spirits mystically depart their bodies; but rather than being in an ecstasy of utter companionship with the woman at his side, Dickey's speaker mounts a private reverie. Formerly "At one with her singing flesh," he is now completely apart from her. The brother-ghost fuses metaphorically with the underground stream as Dickey tries to shift from the simply personal to an image of generalized, archetypal significance. When the narrator turns "from the girl" to the ghost, that aesthetic fulcrum bears the weight of sadness and guilt of the survivor who can be "At one" with a woman, who can lie in the grass in springtime, who can sing his songs, relish his memories, and imagine things that he could never actually have known.

Making poems—those quasi-living things—helps ameliorate the poet's guilt, just as the tricks in "The String" provide a ritual revival of the dead brother. However, the sign that the string-trickster's parents will not be satisfied with artificial reincarnation is also the sign of the limitations of art in general, especially mystical art. And it dredges up once again the debt the poet may feel for not being able to repay his parents for his own mere life.

Some guilt persists in "The Vegetable King," but the poem expounds a more universal guilt, which is the necessary result of all human activity. With yet another speaker sleeping out-of-doors, Dickey emphasizes that the true vegetation-god has always about him the aura of death, which Dickey delineates with a neatly understated imagery of flowers, rather than longer-lived or harvest-yielding plants. Thus reiterating the fatal transience of the vegetation-god and our human immersion in that same mortality, Dickey implies God's complicity in the guilty condition of humankind: "Beneath the gods and animals of Heaven, / Mismade inspiringly, like them, / I fall to a colored sleep." The guilt of the world, then, becomes universally distributed. God is responsible for fecundity, sexuality, the mismaking of constellations and human beings; and in His creations He owns the manifestation of His fertility king, who ominously bears home to wife and son "Magnificent pardon, and dread, impending crime."

Eventually Dickey's personal guilt dissipates, allowing some divine participation in the faults: "In 'The Vegetable King,' I try to mythologize my family; this, I guess, is my answer to Eliot's use of the Osiris myth" (*SI*, 85). For Dickey, his brother is part of spiritual immanence in all life-processes, especially since that particular immanence is inherent in the poet's own coming-to-life. But fairly early in his career Dickey emerged at least partially absolved of the guilt he felt about Eugene. The overt spiritualistic presence of the ghostly dead declined in his poetry until, a decade after the simpler mysticisms of *Into the Stone* and *Drowning with Others* (1962), he had evolved to freshly empowered literary-psychological archetypes, legends, historical allusions, and hard-regained instincts. The patently supernatural almost disappears. Guilt in the later works is most often the result of adult personal and social behavior, a very different thing from the morbidity families lay upon their children, intentionally or not.

Guilt and Survival: The Emblem-Poems of War

If Dickey's brother-guilt was unfair, more so are the claims made upon the general populace by warfare. The "War" poems of *Into the Stone,* however, tend to deal more specifically with the burdens, not of the direct victims of shot and shell, but of the perpetrators, the warriors, a point of view established by Dickey's own experience as a fighter-bomber pilot. Perhaps because of what he calls, in "The Firebombing" (1964), "this detachment, / The honored aesthetic evil," of being literally sky-high above the effects of push-button aerial warfare, Dickey seems to deal more emblematically with war scenes. That is, the narrator within the poem contemplates rational meanings which cluster about a particular image.

But the warrior's vision proves relatively narrow in most of these poems. In later books, *Helmets* (1964) and *Buckdancer's Choice* (1965), Dickey enters into more profound questions about warfare: Who is guilty? What is one man's appropriate response to war's demands on him? What is expected by our ancestors? our comrades? How does one rebuild moral responsibility? sanity? The early poems, however, are concerned with fairly limited, immediate experiences. In most cases, the speaker, caught by circumstances, has free range only in his private mental associations, often in fatigue, or at night. These emblematic poems "fulfill" not by communal rituals, but by giving the poet-narrator an object for meditation and a developing cluster of meanings to parse out:

> Across from him, someone snaps on
> The faceted lights of a cabin.
> There, like the meaning of war, he sees
> A strong, poor diamond of light.

And yet these war poems and their guilt-evasive detachment are oddly more humane than many of the nature poems, perhaps for the sense of troubled reflection, the man not quite sure as to how he does, much less should, respond to such high destruction. In "Sleeping Out at Easter," for instance, the narrator seeks only for himself knowledge and power from nature (or from within), while in "The Jewel" he wants—however vaguely—to be sensitive to other people as well as to things. Later, in "The Firebombing," the point is clearly made—Dickey's terrible recognition of lost, or misplaced, humanity. In "Drinking from a Helmet" (1963) and "Between Two Prisoners" (1960), a strong sense of the impersonal force of war upon individuals drives the poet to social awareness. In the poems about family, it is as though they, too, are something to draw from rather than give to. Although in some poems about his children and in some about women he does assume the role of protector, it is when things are distant and out of hand, as in war, that he seems most in touch with the need for humane attitudes and conduct. In "The Wedding," a more straightforward, less surrealistic poem than "The Jewel," Dickey plays upon the warriors' practice of making artifacts—symbols of and for themselves. In the most mechanized, depersonalized circumstances men still long for gentle arts and precious memories they can sustain: to sew tiger-heads on their jackets, to make rings, to wear jewelry for their wives in their "black-painted aircraft."

Incongruously, one of the war poems reveals a troubling conception of women that is important throughout Dickey's work. The pilot in "The Enclosure" is somewhat passive: "I rested my head . . . the mask fell away." But this passivity is compelled by circumstance, a restraint that results in a perverse, pressurized eroticism: "In retrospect I find that one of the themes in *Into the Stone* is the notion I've always had of a woman as a kind of vision, based upon her inaccessibility" (*SI,* 91). This "idealization of woman" is intensified in wartime when the women are close enough to see but not available to touch. Then, "when the war was over and the soldier moved on to occupation duty, he would have an enormous residue of physical passion, fantasy, and yes, love, and he would give it to the enemy's women, who would be available, again paradoxically, as his own countrymen had never been, during the war" (*SI,* 92). As the pilot tells it, his consummation is to "fall / On the enemy's women / With intact and incredible love." Even he, though, perceives the unbelievableness of "love" for such distant women, who might actually have suffered at some time or other a "fall" of bombs from his plane. This is a conqueror's love, the rapine of the warrior, and, as love, it is "incredible." Finally, the necessary confinement of American nurses behind guards and wire—a fantasy of sexual bondage—is yet another crime of war, even upon men and women in service together. All are victims; most, guilty.

In "The Performance," by far the best of these five war poems, Dickey chooses to give his victim a name. The narrator begins with an easy, colloquial lilt: "The last time I saw Donald Armstrong / He was staggering oddly off into the sun. . . ." But the main story he tells is how the airman "toppled his head off / On an island beach to the south." Now, "months later," he is able "to see him again / In the sun, when I learned how he died, / And imagined him, there. . . ." Not relying on the forces of nature for transcendent revelation, nor on the good offices of ghostly spirits for hypnotic power, nor on poetic indirection and high-eloquent diction, nor on regular meter and incantatory refrain to record the grisly event, Dickey's speaker makes pure and simple narrative rise with emotion and subside into sad clarity—the poignant death of one clearly drawn man with a name, a talent (imperfect gymnastics, but his own), and a friendly Horatio left behind to tell his story.

Unlike "The Enclosure" or "The Jewel," "The Performance" does not turn to the nameless victims (except for the Japanese captors and headsman); the herded soldiers, pilots, and nurses; the inconvenienced, bereft wives at home—all in general. It details the small-scale heroism of one man who had to die but who courageously determined to impose his own ritual. An amateur gymnast, Armstrong made his last gesture, his last self-definition, by performing hand-stands and the kip-up to the astonishment of his "small captors" before he "knelt down in himself / Beside his hacked, glittering grave, having done / All things in this life that he could." The narrator, not directly involved in the deadly events, stands as the voice-over, the rememberer, the imagining admirer of this man-symbol of desperate grace.

Death, and Others

After the bravura of "The Performance," and trusting the thematic logic of having "Death, and Others" follow "War," a reader might have expected great things of *Into the Stone*'s third section; but only half those six poems are very good. Dickey omitted "Uncle," "Poem," and "The Sprinter's Sleep" from *Poems: 1957–1967*. And he was right. Neither "Poem" nor "Uncle" achieves the resonant portraiture even of such close-to-the-vest works as "Mangham" (1965) and "The Leap" (1967), not to mention the extraordinary treatments of individuals in "Falling" and "May Day Sermon." But the next three pieces are successively more sure-handed and, coincidentally, more affirmative. It is as though, with "Death" progressively and properly domesticated and mythologized, the poet may be left free to contemplate vital connections—"Love"—in his final section.

"The Other," one of the most ambitious poems in "Death, and Others," portrays the ghostly brother-figure in self-consciously mythic terms. Dickey has said that he "liked poems which had a basis of narrative" and that he "worked most fruitfully in cases in which there was no clear-cut distinction between what was actually happening and what was happening in the mind of a character in the poem" (*BB*, 287). Dickey's Other is at least in part the narrator himself, as he indicates in the first lines of the poem: "Holding onto myself by the hand, / I change places into the spirit / I had as a rack-ribbed child. . . ." The narrator's language shifts rather quickly from present to past tense references, thus accentuating the overwhelming force of the experience upon the speaker. "Reason," he says, "fell from my mind at a touch." The result of such abandonment of the intellect in favor of the spirit is that the narrator not only envisions but also identifies with his brother-spirit and finally with an almost Ovidian form of ancient divinity: the bull-man-god. Philosophically, this confrontation with the spirit-world, with nature, and with the mythic archetypes leads the narrator to a somewhat cynical, world-weary striving for more life, for more capacity to prolong dying. It is a curious mix of common-sense physical exercise and the recognition that such care ultimately ends in the grave. The Other in this poem, then, takes hold of the narrator, inspires him with transcendent glory, and leaves him in the tree-bound scene, which also will "cast down its foliage with the years."

Dickey wants unrestrained access—transcendent connections—to all things natural, and that aspiration requires his almost evangelical disloca- tion of normal sensual and intellectual conditions. In "Trees and Cattle" the poet says, "in some earthly way / I have been given my heart." But there are also unearthly perceptions, somewhat analogous to those in "The Other." The mythologizing impulse is seen in similar references to Heaven, to spiritual gold-value, to bull-bodies, and to bird-wing apotheoses. In "Trees and Cattle" ecstasy is better rendered because the speaker maintains a consistent present-tense point of view, thus reinforc- ing the reader's belief in the currency and immediacy of the experience. But paradox also helps to evoke a sense of ecstasy. The speaker in "The Other" uses a bird and a bull to distinguish between the spiritual presence of the dead brother and the physical presence of the narrator-as-youth. In "Trees and Cattle," though, the two major images fuse in one figure—a paradox compounded when the tree takes on bird wings at the end of the poem.

Obviously, Dickey allegorizes some transcendent reality: the *things* in the poems are signs. As earlier he brought himself to measure against T. S. Eliot's Osiris myth, here he considers something like Eliot's "still point of the turning world" ("Burnt Norton," 1. 64), a metaphysical contradiction that tries to unify space, time, and eternity in one indescribable concept.

As Dickey works in these "Death, and Others" poems to confirm his necessary sense of wholeness, his ultimate paradox is to maintain earthli- ness and spirituality at once. In that pursuit in "Trees and Cattle" he turns his vision around from mysticism to "some earthly way" only to return at the very end to a tree that "leaps up / On wings that could save me from death." The speaker runs from ecstatically vegetative—treelike—to bovine, and then to spiritual—without form—all in a rush of paradox, counting on his readers to hold the rush at once in mind and memory.

The fantasizing in "Trees and Cattle" about the wings of trees palls next to the more brilliant images of "The Other"; but both poems, for their too-conscious literariness and their resultant denaturalizing of images, are very different from later Dickey poems, like "Kudzu," which touch the power but do not violate the phenomenological integrity of their plants and animals.

"Walking on Water" depicts the confusion of elements in the illusion that a boy on a plank in the water is supernaturally supported, in the view of those who do not see the plank. The reader, however, is immediately let in on the secret, made aware of the facts of the illusion, and spared the embarrassment of interpreting the scene as the seabirds do. The walk itself is a thing of glory: the illusion that one could actually be upheld by the fluid elements is stripped and then reclothed in mystery for the poet's audience: the boy seems to be conjuring the incredulous seabirds.

Even for the natural birds, though, something unseen and ominous looms at the end of the poem, transformed, like the vision of what human beings can and cannot do upon the ocean's surface: "A huge, hammerheaded spirit / Shall pass, as if led by the nose into Heaven." However grandiose or whimsical that illusion may appear to be, its depiction of the boy-poet himself as emblem, seeing himself and then extemporizing, almost rhapsodizing, about his own appearance, shakes the readers loose from their expectations of order, self-control, and common perspective.

Love, the Naturalistic Sacrament

The "Love" poems of *Into the Stone* use nature images very safely, conventionally suggestive: making love is like being on water ("The Landfall" and "Awaiting the Swimmer"); moonlight is the transforming agent of lovers' visions ("Near Darien"). Nature images here are mostly decoration, emblems, not in themselves conduits of knowledge and power. As a group, however, the "Love" poems are a modest culmination of the various unions effected through Dickey's sensitive, energetic attention to experience: i.e., family, war, and death.

In the later, comic poem "Cherrylog Road" (1963), love is primarily a matter of comic exuberance and uncontainable youthful bounty. In poems of more delicate ambitions, Dickey is subtler in identifying sex with profound—even cosmic—natural motions. He often associates the movement of water, for instance, with erotically portrayed women, e.g. "Root-Light, or the Lawyer's Daughter" (1969), "The Night Pool" (1965), "Coming Back to America" (1965), and, from *Into the Stone,* "Awaiting the Swimmer." In this last poem, the "moves of her body" are "fear-killing," and her motions therefore ameliorate the ultimate fear, of death. The poem is not simplistic, however. The river's motion inspires both the swimmer and the onlooker-lover, but an unresolved threat is in

"The midst of the road where she's buried." Clearly, one must "keep swimming" or die, keep moving (making love) or be static forever.

The poem implies a strong ego in Dickey's narrator ("I love / That moving-to-me love"), but it also concludes with a knell of inadequacy that is rare in Dickey men: "What can I perform, to come near her? / How hope to bear up, when she gives me / The fear-killing moves of her body?" It is difficult to judge if the speaker is fearful about his ability to sustain and match the love-making moves that come with primal force from the river through the woman to him; or if there is an overpowering sense of commitment, of obligation and responsibility, of gratitude, to the woman who comes thus to him, without fear in herself and implicitly demanding that he participate in that same fearlessness.

Most esteemed by Dickey among dauntless lover-heroes is Orpheus, who dared enter the underworld to retrieve his beloved Eurydice from the dead. Unhappily, in "Orpheus Before Hades," Dickey placed his own best instincts under some weary preconceptions about mythic imagery. He plays to his strengths when he is "working both semi-consciously and quite consciously toward mythologizing my own factual experience" (*SI*, 85), not when he is plainly shopping in a traditional mythological storehouse. Wisely, Dickey omitted this poem, too, from *Poems 1957–1967*.

"On the Hill Below the Lighthouse" is typical of what William J. Martz calls "distinctive voice."[6] The reader again has a definite sense of a speaker with a personality, an identifiable situation—not a usual place for love-making, but one that anyone might visualize immediately upon the poet's description. The poem's refrain is of the cumulative sort that Dickey uses so well, the last line of every stanza being gathered to compose the last stanza. The crossing over of these stanza-concluding lines is analogous to the synaesthesia that Dickey manipulates so cleanly throughout the poem, the outer and inner worlds mingling with seductive ease.

The narrator's perspective from below the lighthouse, but on a hill, gives a slant, off-center view to complement the periodic light from the regulated beam of the lighthouse. The poet moves easily through personifications, through unnatural juxtapositions with almost slangy language: "The sun is dead, thinking of night / Swung round like a thing on a chain." The daring generality of "thing" is a signal that just-talking operates here. Most of the time, Dickey's best effect is to evoke the highest poetic insight with the language that people actually use. In a way, even the repeated lines, following the style of epic singers and careful preachers, acknowledge the listening populace rather than a gaggle of cloistered readers.

"Near Darien" is a love poem whose sonorous language and oracular tone mediate between the hard, specific images of the speaker out in a wooden boat, riding the soft waves of a tidal flats region, through the night, with whatever soft risks that such sleeping might entail with regard to weather or other mischance. The incantatory distance of the poet is accentuated by the speaker's physical separation from his loved ones on shore. The distance that is clear from our observations of his mental state is quite simply embodied in his distance from his wife, who finally rises as if by magic in the air, herself part of some concatenation of forces from the water, air, and moon, to bring them together. He speaks of his own power as being from the sun: "She shall stand to her knees in her shadow, / Gazing outward, her eyes unshaded, / / As I ride blindly home from the sun"; while the moon acts as a romantic transmogrifier: "I lie down, / Beginning to sleep, sustained / By a huge, ruined stone in the sky." The boat is the vehicle of his spiritual voyage (without the overblown derivativeness of "Orpheus Before Hades"), and the voyage is out of reason: "Not wishing to know how she came there, / Commanded by glorious powers." The time seems unreal, but it brings a man straining out of the sun home to a woman who simultaneously seeks him.

"Into the Stone," unlike many title poems, does confirm the tone of the book, whose meditative inwardness is especially noticeable when contrasted with the social concerns of *Drowning with Others* (1962). The "stone" is often the moon: "Near Darien" calls it "a huge, ruined stone in the sky." And to go into the stone is to go upward, with the Platonic implications of our desiring to escape mere fleshly reality to attain to the higher, truer, spiritual reality. At the same time, the poet implies going downward, into the earthiness of geologic stones, paradoxically so old they serve as a kind of concrete timelessness.

"Into the Stone" is also—not to forget—a love poem, telling how a man's idea of himself—and, by inference, a woman's idea of herself and of the man—*is* their reality. The speaker alludes to having given up his parents in the age-old theme of leaving parents to cleave to the woman, but the poet's main idea is that human love is very like the mystical union a person can feel with nature. Love becomes almost a naturalistic sacrament. In this early-career poem, it is never quite clear what mystic knowledge the lovers gain. Later, with "May Day Sermon," Dickey undertakes to show explicitly how natural powers, as seen in pagan fertility traditions, interact with the social forces of American Protestantism. But "Into the Stone" does not take on so expansive nor so didactic an issue. Even a worldly, cynical person may wistfully or heroically aspire to some limitless concourse with the dead past and the mythic cosmos: "The dead have their chance in my body. / The stars are drawn into their myths." But, from its simple opening ("On the way to a woman, I give / My heart all the way into moonlight"), through a mysterious suspension of natural law ("No thing that shall die as I step / May fall"), the poem curves into graceful acceptance of human finitude: "I bear nothing but moonlight upon me. / I am known; I know my love." This speaker is secure at the end— connected.

The concluding lines' humility and clarity gain power as a result of the myth that has preceded them, the sense of suprareality that informs this superficial world with meaning. But these last two lines make it plain that the poet is one whose image of himself and of his lover is both empirically verifiable and spiritually vital. It is not enough to gloss the last line with the " 'biblical' (you know) kind of knowledge" when it is conspicuous that Dickey is stressing that the knowledge lovers have permeates their world. It has virtually nothing to do with what we commonly call religion; however, it is tightly joined with, inseparable from, the natural spiritual immanence that Dickey urges us to recognize for our own well-being.

"The Landfall," the last poem in *Into the Stone,* is about two lovers who pull a boat to a landfall and then make love. Its simple story line allows the poet to count on his readers' understanding at least those bare bones at the end of his book. The trouble is (and Dickey apparently saw the weakness, since he also excluded this one from *Poems 1957–1967*), "The Landfall" does not evoke the mystic assent of works like "Into the Stone" or "Near Darien," nor does it pack the narrative punch of "The Performance."

One of the most disturbing elements of this poem, however—and it designates an issue of Dickey's developing concept of love—is the implication that the male provides all the language and, therefore, all the real understanding of the lovers' experience. In "Into the Stone," by way of contrast, the two are equally involved; thus their love scene is persuasive—even if one is not credulous of mystical communion between distant lovers. "The Landfall" prefigures "Blood" (1969), in which Dickey's narrator is totally in charge although—frighteningly, one assumes, for the woman—he does not even know where he is when he wakes up. The time of their passion is lost in the oblivion of drunkenness, and the speaker's assertion that she is "safe" with him is specious, since his own alertness is in doubt from the first lines:

> In the cold night
> Of somebody. Is there other
> Breath? What did I say?
> Or do?

The theme of "The Landfall" is similar, without the implicit chaos but still condescending to the woman. Dickey's men are generally in charge of their love poems, and, even as they seek enlightenment and grace, they often overbear.

In "Birches," Robert Frost says, "Earth's the right place for love: / I don't know where it's likely to go better." His echo continues through Dickey's work, constituting a major theme. Thirteen of the twenty-four poems in *Into the Stone* contain the word itself, but Dickey uses "love" so broadly (and surprisingly often) that it has little constancy except in the sense of "connection," a gloss that figures prominently in "The Sheep Child" and its commentary in *Self-Interviews*. "Power and Light" (1967), in fact, has as its epigraph, "only connect," from that of E. M. Forster's novel *Howard's End*. Perhaps the term is used differently in "Apollo" (I. *For the First Manned Moon Orbit,* 1969), where the love described is world-wide, an earth-unique thing, as Dickey strongly believes that this planet is the only place where life exists in the universe:

> And behold
>
> The blue planet steeped in its dream
>
> Of reality, its calculated vision shaking with
> The only love.

While Randall Jarrell, in "The Death of the Ball Turret Gunner" (1945), could write of his doomed airman, "Six miles from earth, loosed from its dream of life,"[7] Dickey's much more distant astronaut can see that earth's dream of love is as real as life itself.

"The Energized Man"

In his introduction to *Into the Stone* in 1960, John Hall Wheelock writes about personality before he even considers the "good workmanship" of the poets included in that volume of *Poets of Today.* And to emphasize Dickey's distinctive personality is in no way to disparage his insights or his craft.

Even his most supportive readers, though, seem to downplay the particularity of this poet in the interest of claiming his universality. But it is almost too easy to speak of poets who can cruise through universals, who can identify great order beyond the seeming chaos, etc., as, for instance, Michael Goldman, in the *Nation:* "Dickey gives the moment a natural energy, not the energy of the poet's insistence upon his own personality but the energy of a vast life outside the poet which moves all things through one another and through him."[8] It is almost as if the predictable charge against romantic "Hemingway Heroism" or "Boy Scout Machismo" prompts the well-intentioned defense of denying Dickey's true interest in the pure self, what Gerard Manley Hopkins called the poet's "selving." The fact is, as Wheelock has written, "Personality . . . implies originality. True originality is unconscious."[9] In his essays "The Poet Turns on Himself" (1966) and "The Energized Man" (1979), Dickey advocates individuals' qualities rather than those of the masses, "universals," as they are popularly conceived. This poet intends to show what is possible to awakened human beings so that they may never again be satisfied with "drift" and "inconsequence,"[10] that they may heed the energetic poet who makes himself so painfully available to their scrutiny. Dickey's poetry is not *only* about himself, of course; he is a very identifiable individual who *also* leads us into worldly experiences. In this recognition of our common human condition, the second book, *Drowning with Others,* steps into new Dickey territory.

Chapter Three
Reaching Out to Others

To speak of the poet's stance, his personality, in the second book is perhaps abstract and inexact, but Dickey becomes a more self-accepted, assertive actor instead of the relatively passive observer. Repeatedly, in *Into the Stone,* with poems like "The Call," "The Vegetable King," "The Sprinter's Sleep," and "The Other," Dickey's narrator is overwhelmed by Something Out Yonder. *Drowning with Others* (1962) proceeds with more confidence, less mincing (probably too strong a word) than that first book. It is as though the poet found his calling, to transliterate the experiences of the physical world into the physical symbols of poetry.

The Solitary Self Is Not Enough

In *Drowning with Others,* Dickey extends and develops the themes of *Into the Stone,* but one consideration emerges with particular emphasis: social interconnection. With the first poem of the book, "The Lifeguard," mutual responsibility is made clear: the familiar guilt motif is made a social affair. Having lost a child to the dark lake, the fallen hero retreats from the silent accusation of the children who once saw him as godlike and who consequently felt utterly safe while he was on duty. Like the protagonist in a later poem, "Power and Light," this lifeguard feels that he must escape from people and try to recover in solitude when things have gone wrong. His self-esteem prior to his failure seems to have depended much upon his responsibility to society. During his retreat, at night, he envisions a mystical child arising from the lake, smiling. At the end, however, reality asserts itself, and the lifeguard is left hopelessly to "hold in my arms a child / Of water, water, water."

Dickey pursues his nature theme in the society of hunters in "Listening to Foxhounds," which begins in the full fellowship of the hunt. The men sit around campfires, listening to their "brothers," the hounds. Then the focus draws down to one man whose dog has made his own remarkable sound. The omniscient-seeming point of view is unusual for Dickey, but the voice gradually shifts to the second person: "You know which chosen man has heard." The poem's most wondrous effect is in merging the social group of fox-hunters with the singular narrator (who obfuscates himself in the second person) and with the almost spiritual identity of men with hounds, who, in their pursuit, have their own identity with the foxes. The men strain emotionally together, competitively hoping to recognize their own hounds even as they try to conceal unmanly enthusiasm. This reticent single-mindedness about one's own dog redoubles the tension when, "if one should do so," the narrator "might" imagine the fox. Fully aware of his comrades' social pressure, the speaker must be even more self-contained than in awaiting public joy over his dog: "Who runs with the fox / Must sit here like his own image, / Giving nothing of himself. . . ." He imagines that his private musings are more energized, more intense, and more mysterious than those of the other hunters; but their society is essential to his imaginative experience.

"Between Two Prisoners" allows for a social connection like the hunter's with the victimized fox, but its ambiguity as to who the prisoners are plays out Dickey's preference for narration that intermingles what is inside with what is outside the speaker of the poem. As with "The Performance," the narrator takes into account not only the American prisoners and their feelings but also the condition (and eventual death) of at least one of the Japanese guards. The schoolroom setting is significant as the prisoners and their captors are separated by force in a building where society normally teaches how to connect through civilized traditions. With prisoners immobilized, "A belief in words grew upon them / That the unbound, who walk, cannot know." Once, in this place, children communicated by "deep, hacked hieroglyphics" in their school desks, or through "the luminous chalks of all colors" with which they adorned the classroom; but now "The guard . . . leaned close / . . . To hear in a foreign tongue, / All things which cannot be said." Later, as the small guard is hanged "In a closed horse stall in Manila . . . / No one knows what language he spoke / As his face changed into all colors." The villain, as in "The Enclosure," is war itself, whose villainy includes the perversion of the high social virtue of language: "Speaking words that can never be spoken / Except in a foreign tongue, / In the end, at the end of a war."

"A View of Fujiyama After the War" also depicts unanticipated connections among military enemies. The poem shows, with only moderate success, the ambiguities inherent in defeat and victory. Foreshadowing "The Firebombing," Dickey's social theme here is ironic, since the poem tells what the poet has *not* had to suffer—the indignity of being (figuratively) alive again only because the enemy lives and can write poems on foreign soil. The poet's guilt is partly for his cannibalism of his and others' lives.

Brothers: Living and Dead

Although its role is much reduced, Dickey's brother-ghost persists in *Drowning with Others*. "In the Tree House at Night" deals both with Dickey's older, deceased brother, Eugene, and with his younger, surviving one; while "Armor" concentrates on the brother-ghost, so vividly construed earlier in "The Underground Stream," "The String," and "The Other."

In portraying the brother-guilt, "Armor" comes to more mature resolution than some earlier poems. Its main image—the speaker's donning armor—corresponds to Dickey's putting on a boar's head in "Approaching Prayer" (1964), to having a life-mask made and suffering eye-burn and temporary blindness just prior to writing the "Cahill Is Blind" section of *Alnilam* (Dickey's novel in progress), and perhaps even to playing helmeted football in high school and college. Dickey is a willful mind-mover: he likes imposing environmental (or apparel) changes to enhance his imagination. In "Falling," the stewardess, thrown suddenly out of a plane's door, removes her clothes as she descends, thus intentionally to alter herself "beyond explanation" before she hits the ground. Conversely altering himself by putting armor on—which normally makes a person less vulnerable—Dickey's speaker becomes strangely more vulnerable. He imagines the shell as having "the power of the crab and the insect," suggesting that he is better able to survive certain physical onslaughts. But he chiefly turns the armor into a self-reflexive mirror. It forces him inward and causes him to call up the encompassing spirit of his dead brother, "whose features I knew / / By the feel of their strength on my face / And whose limbs by the shining of mine." It is the brother again, but with a somewhat different mission than before. In this poem he merges spiritually with the narrator, becoming a sort of infused sponsor for his entry into Heaven. There is no guilt, only opportunity. When this poem is done, the speaker no longer feels that his life will be constantly enthralled by the memory or spirit of his brother. Now, by abandoning the armor to stand by itself in the woods as a symbol of his brother, waiting separate and apart from the speaker, this more reconciled man comes to the place in his life where he is able to imagine meeting his brother, taking on his shell again as a glowing energy-field in the woods—but only after death, only at the time of eternal union. Enabled by this armorial vision, the narrator can put the brother aside, live his own life to its end, rejoin his brother (if their immortality should prove to commingle), and investigate the mystical armor to see "What man is within to live with me / When I begin living forever."

"In the Tree House at Night" is an effort to expunge brother-guilt by acting out the spirit's commands, of playfully indulging useful, constructive energies. But the play confirms serious relations both with the ghostly dead and with nature. It calls for the poet to make full contact with society other than the wandering spirits. The poet's preoccupation with mere survivorship has here been much diverted, and the poem's almost blatant sexuality (stanzas 6–8) would indicate that the poet is less guilt-ridden than gratified by his brother.

The narrator assumes sensual but vegetative traits:

> My green graceful bones fill the air
> With sleeping birds. Alone, alone
> And with them I move gently.
> I move at the heart of the world.

As in "The Vegetable King," Dickey keeps his plant imagery vague, thus leaving himself free to use his trees as media for sporadic returns. Dickey appears to want his trees primarily to bear a message rather than to be specific, real things. As in "Fog Envelops the Animals," trees are subject to transformation, whereas animals in early poems are rarely so altered. Later, in "The Sheep Child," "Madness" (1969), "For the Last Wolverine," and the two "Reincarnation" poems, as he stretches for extraordinary insights, his creatures also become extraordinary, even to the limit of creating a *delirium tremens* lobster for *The Zodiac* (1976).

In resorting to images of trees rather than people, or even animals, Dickey runs a risk of losing contact with his readers, but his formidable rhetoric compensates. To begin with "And" solicits the reader's assent that he was already somehow with the poet before he began. But even with a solicitous beginning, Dickey's first line draws the reader up short: "And now the green household is dark." Having been enticed into the *a priori* narrative, then brought abruptly to a halt by a one-line opening sentence, the subjugated reader is chastened to accept a deliberate, meditative description, as though the reader himself had rustled about and settled in to spend the night in a tree house. Dickey attends closely to the details of nature ("The half-moon completely is shining / On the earth-lighted tops of the trees"), and the reader is seduced to the narrator's physical perspective, there to accept the speaker's isolation even as the brothers are paradoxically also present:

> We lie here like angels in bodies,
> My brothers and I, one dead,
> The other asleep from much living,
>
> In mid-air huddled beside me.

"Hunting Civil War Relics at Nimblewill Creek" also portrays a brother-companion, but this one is alive and helping the narrator search old battlefields with a metal-detector. Both youngsters are descendants and therefore survivors of the men in the terrible war almost a century before. Their closeness is important because it is partly through seeing his brother's face transmit the influence of the dead that the speaker gains insight into the battleground. The spirits rise from within the dormant things buried in the earth and integrate with living society. The speaker feels communion with his "one brother," but he also senses that the brother is a spiritual conduit, a human analogue to the metal-detector: the machine identifies and reveals the lost "mess tin or bullet" while the living instrument—the brother—rears up the ancestral spirits.

Fathers and Children

There are many more poems about father-child than about sibling relationships in *Drowning with Others:* "The Owl King," "Dover: Believing in Kings," "To His Children in Darkness," "The Hospital Window," "The Magus," "Antipolis," and "Facing Africa." The trend represents a broadening, if not a maturing, of the poet's concerns. The responsibility of a parent for his or her child is highly significant to Dickey's growing social concerns.

"The Call," of *Into the Stone,* builds upon three major images: the father—who speaks these lines—the blind son, and the owl king. Obviously unsatisfied with his treatment of the subject in one poem, Dickey came later to include "The Call" as Part I of "The Owl King," in *Drowning with Others.* The poem is technically interesting for its dislocation of everyday reality and its entry into a mythical, magical world not seen in Dickey's work anywhere else. With the father calling after his son, who is lost in the woods of the owl king, Dickey misdirects the reader not so much to castigate the father's wrongheadedness as to indicate the vastness and difficulty of mystical knowledge. The reader is in awe of what surrounds the speaker, not pitying or condescending. The father's (and the reader's) inklings here are of the see-through-a-glass-darkly sort, later to be fully known through the owl and the son. "The Call' moves like a question, with the father wondering as to the source and composition of his own calling sound. Dickey could not let such ambiguities rest, later enlisting the owl king and finally the son for substantial clarification in two additional sections to the poem.

However it might first have begun to stir in his mind as an exploration of parental responsibility, "The Owl King" is one of Dickey's most completely spiritualistic and animistic poems. Although its finished three parts are specifically assigned to father, son, and owl king (echoes of Father, Son, and Holy Ghost are deafening), the poem is actually about the interlocking—even the interchangeability—of the myriad spirits of the world. Seeking the blind child, the father is not only immersed in his own sounds but also attuned to nature. He knows that true knowledge proceeds from feeling: "I fee. the deep dead turn / My blind child round toward my calling."

Dickey sets reader and father on a mystical journey by the illogicality of the setting: "Through the trees, with the moon underfoot, / More soft than I can, I call." The search for something spiritual, in artistic terms, is nearly allegorical, a mode Dickey returns to later, with "The Eye-Beaters" (1968) and *The Zodiac* (1976). And so the owl king, no regular bird, is somewhat like Plato's philosopher who has left the cave to peer painfully at the sun and then to return with unimagined truths to persuade his benighted (and hostile) fellows. But this excursion into sunlight has a different effect:

> At last I opened my eyes
> In the sun, and saw nothing there.
> That night I parted my lids
> Once more, and saw dark burn
> Greater than sunlight or moonlight,
> For it burned from deep within me.

With claws tight upon the limbs, embedded and needing to be "prised up," the owl king is plugged into nature, empowered by it from within.

More than the human father, the owl king is an active creator: "I swore to myself," he says, and "Every light was too feeble to show / My world as I knew it must be." He must make the world according to his own vision: "I heard what I listened to hear." Since the owl is not human, his voice, creative though it be, is inadequate to the clear expression of his own insights. But his vision ("all but my seeing had failed") leads him to the child, who, when found, becomes unified with the owl in their response to the father's searching call. The blind child learns, by some mystical apprehension, the action of the owl's "blazing, invented eyes." He learns to constitute—or reconstitute—each living thing by its own special quality, "Each waiting alive in its own / Peculiar light to be found."

Part II signals that Dickey has no illusions that it is better to be an owl. The blind son is described by the owl himself as possessing great powers: "Every tree's life lived in his fingers." But the owl king at the end of Part II asserts his superiority as the creative fulcrum of the poem, while the human beings play off the steady center of the owl. The father calls for the son; the owl king mediates; and the son assimilates it all. The conclusion of Part II makes it clear that the child's mind is imaginatively bound and directed by the owl king, but it is compelled to the end of regaining his father. The owl king is a dream, however much he may be the willful and "ruling passion."

Part III, "The Blind Child's Story," is consistently different in diction and rhythm from Parts I and II, which more closely resemble each other. Part III opens with emphasis on the youth of the speaker: "I am playing going down / In my weight lightly, / Down, down the hill." Here Dickey is able to reexperience the senses in a way that we often associate with a child's startlingly fresh outlook: "A leaf falls on me, / It must be a leaf I hear it / Be thin against me." The lines rush on, as if the poet were to imagine the constant flow of sensual messages through the body of a blind child; and the unconventional syntax, comma-spliced, fused, and enjambed, helps to convey the image movement.

> . . . and now
> The ground is level,
> It moves it is not ground,
> My feet flow cold
> And wet, and water rushes
> Past as I climb out.

When the first stanza concludes, "I own the entire world," the reader's assent is virtually assured because the child is not able to visualize the limits and demarcations in which sighted persons continuously acquiesce: "It closes a little: the sky / Must be cold, must be giving off / Creatures

that stand here." The child senses the constellations which so entice
Dickey's interest in other poems, the celestial influences that generate
things in this fleshly world; and the boy becomes assertive: "I say they
shine one way." He confirms the phenomenological substance of the
things he can sense: "Trees they are trees around me, / Leaves branch and
bark." But the child's apprehension of himself is more than as a receptor of
sensations to confirm worldly objects. He is said by "someone," he tells us,
to "seem to be blessing them."

As the boy recounts his claw-in-hand greeting of the owl, he says what
perhaps only a child might believably say in such extraordinary circumstances: "Nothing is strange where we are." That is, as the child is
deprived of his "highest" sense—sight—he is also set loose from many
adult limitations as to how the world impinges upon him. Touch and
hearing, for instance, are more immediate, primitive, less mediated
avenues between the Me and the Not-Me.

The owl is acknowledged as Mentor: "I learn from the master of sight /
What to do when the sun is dead." But the real energies originate within
the things perceived: ". . . to make the great darkness work / As it wants
of itself to work." The child envisions a fox and a shining serpent, earlier
described by the owl as "the snake in the form of all life." Another lesson
comes as the fox strikes, and "a small thing / Being caught, cries
out. . . ." This sudden shock of violent death in the woods enables the
child to make another essential connection: "How beings and sounds go
together; / I understand / The voice of my singing father." The mortal cry
of the "small thing" is enough for the boy to grasp the grief of his father,
too. The human child's assimilative mind prevails, and he descends to
regain the real world, now transformed to some extent by his new insights.
After such transcendence and descent, some residual insight remains:
"The wood comes back in a light / It did not know it withheld." The boy's
understanding has deepened; he has perceived the source of perception to
be within the things perceived. He has learned to interact with the real
world by practicing the imaginative dream-magic of the owl king. The
child is able to connect at last with his father, caught up now in that
natural world newly and brilliantly seen by the blind son. Even the owl,
now, has been assimilated by the child to some degree of identity with the
father: "Far off, the owl king / Sings like my father, growing / In power."
And the child, newfound—but mostly to and by himself—closes the
poem affirmatively, confidently, having inherited some energies of the
father as well as the owl king.

"To His Children in Darkness" foreshadows another projection of Dickey's imagination into the dark: "The Eye-Beaters." In both poems, the narrator imagines what someone else knows in darkness: in the early poem, his children's dreams are invented; in "The Eye-Beaters," the institutionalized blind children's primordial visions are imagined. The blind children (in their kind of darkness) strike and bruise their faces in hopes of rendering some sensation of light, some optic glimmer by the force of blows. It is the adults—the father and the visitor—who create the images and attribute them to the children. From their inspiration, each adult narrator then can probe his own imagination to make sense of the finite human condition and thus can extend its limits through imaginative effort.

The father and the son in "Facing Africa" have no such high aesthetic or archetypally loaded experience together. The poem is somewhat like "A Dog Sleeping on My Feet" as the speaker draws some natural, connective energy from the ocean near his feet. Not even physically touching the water or the boats lying "at rest," the man and his son are linked to them by the "long, / Warm, dangling shadows" of their legs as they are seated on the "stone jetties." The son's presence is important in this poem because it provides a handle of social and familial behavior to allow the narrator a check on his poetic enthusiasm, his seeking after knowledge without the brake of social scrutiny. The son also gives the father social affirmation, a necessary balance here as it is in "A Dog Sleeping on My Feet" and, later, in "Slave Quarters." Responsibility and true hopefulness are embodied in the offspring, and, in this case, the son has even come to participate in the imagining, the new knowing, of the father.

"Antipolis" is of an almost equally exotic context as Africa, for this American poet. The poem is of the "Guggenheim" variety, *de rigueur* for those who have traveled expressly for the purpose of becoming authors. The Greek city, the "powder-blue ocean," the son reading Greek, and the poet's self-image as multi-spirited, all are elements to play on the foreignness of the scene to jar the naive American loose to hold more sophisticated concepts and imagery: "I hear in my voice two children, / My son and my soul, / Sing to each other through ages." The poem delves briefly into the theme of potentiality when, at the beginning, the poet feels himself looked "clear through" by the things around him, particularly the market-place squids, hanging for purchase, whose eyes "deepen" and "hold me brightly." The poet is surrounded by perceptions and perceivers, by the ancient dead and the living son, all focused upon and invigorated by his own singing self. His sense of potentiality is incorporated in the son with him: his hope of continuance is at least in part embodied in that vibrant son of his flesh.

A much longer work than most of Dickey's early poems, "Dover: Believing in Kings," uses the persons of father and mother; but the mother is yet only pregnant, and the son is imagined as the son of a king, the father a king, all participating in the mythically accoutred place imagined by the narrator at Dover Beach. This elaborate poem, a glowing rather than a blazing thing, allows, by its length and its simply beautiful tones, the poet to draw together several of his major themes.

The first line sets us hard upon the earth with the speaker and his wife driving off the boat to settle firmly upon land after having crossed the English Channel. The minor mythology of greased swimmers, a mythology particularly fondly held after the exploits of the World War II underwater demolition teams, clamoring like lemmings through the waters, sets the tone for exploring other, more profound myths. As with many of Dickey's speakers, this one's recollection of, or longing for, the marathon swimmer points up a kind of deficiency in himself, a recognition by the person who had crossed in a car on a boat, very unheroically. But such is only a hint, for the speaker learns that his own strengths are more in his sensitive intelligence (Dickey says, "If my poetry has done anything, it has resulted in an increase of both sensitivity and drama in American poetry," *S,* 90) than in his physical stamina and courage: "Within a wind, a wind sprang slowly up."

Dickey's speaker ultimately turns to tell of himself as a king. The weathering gray of Dover merges with the birds and sea, shifting at last to royal images. The grandeur and majesty of the scene produce associations of the stern, gray effort of birds casting themselves (like Hopkins's windhover) against the "airstream of the cliffs," their breasts bearing the gray assault, and then, almost miraculously, the king emerges to the overwhelming awe even of the birds: "*In a moment you cannot imagine / Of air, the gulls fall, shaken.*" With this imagery of royalty and his wife pregnant with a son imagined to be Arthur, the narrator makes a poem to be a call to high intellectual and spiritual refinement, to displace the clunking tourism of the opening lines. As birds move along the line of the cliffs, the people below follow along, feeling majestic enough to comprehend "the balancement of light / *The king wears newly, in singing.*" The poem is much of joy but also of solemnity; its measured, alternating iambs and anapests recall the rhythms of high-eloquent speech, of oratory without bombast.

As finely tuned as "Dover: Believing in Kings" is, its solemnity strikes the serious pose of the poet whose skills are there but whose idea of poetry has not yet matured to the unforced idiosyncrasy of the distinctive James Dickey. "The Magus," published two years after "Dover," invokes by its very title those austere magi-makers of the twentieth century—T. S. Eliot and W. B. Yeats. But Dickey's poem wants to work in two directions at once: to dispel the conventional magi-mystery and to call up the natural mystery of all human life. "This child," he concludes, "is no more than a child." But by this twentieth and last line, the poem has practiced an hypnotic two-line stanza form whose lines are almost all heavily end-stopped, and whose parallel structures of various kinds all work to the benefit of ritual sounds, of almost liturgical pace, and of the puzzlement that any parent may feel at the claim of one Holy Child to be more holy than one's own. The "two / long-lost other men [who] shall be drawn / Slowly up to the brink of the house," recall, of course, the two other magi. But they also, in this poem, reintroduce the ghostly dead imagery, our shadowy close and infinitely distant ancestors. The poem is less powerful than it seems to want to be, and its cautious understatement, even with the late peak of three rhetorical questions, succumbs to paralysis. It is just not enough for the poet to say to himself, "An event more miraculous yet / / Is the thing I am shining to tell you." The shining is never bright enough to break the shell of controlled intellect in this poem: the child never quite ascends to his own glory. So the father's allegations are hollow.

As much as he accomplishes by projecting imagined dreams into children, by symbolically journeying with his son over shadowy seas to Africa, by drinking and roaring his way through Antipolis for his son's enrichment, by meditating through a verbal symphony at Dover, or by starkly undercutting the high religious ambience of the magi, Dickey comes in these poems about fathers and children to speak most plainly and most effectively in "The Hospital Window." An anomaly like "The Performance" among the war poems of *Into the Stone,* "The Hospital Window" reiterates the theme of survivorship—not, as with Donald Armstrong, through some heroic gesture—this time to survive, with a mixture of grief and joy, one's own father. As is common in early Dickey poems, this one begins with a momentarily puzzling dislocation. The speaker's descent in an elevator is deliberately obscured to assure the author the purest sort of control over the reader's expectations and observations: "I have just come down from my father. / Higher and higher he lies / Above me. . . ." The second stanza begins with the repetition, "Still feeling my father ascend," and thus the poet creates the illusion of the father's impending death, his rising away, as into heaven, as the son sinks away from him.

With all the exterior windows glazed by sunlight for the son's view from out in the street, he moves around to catch sight of his father and thus moves almost obliviously into the automobile traffic. The clamorous near-death of the street, the horn-blowing and the outrage, serve to emphasize the vitality of the son, who has only the hope of a silent fatherly wave from a hospital window, a wave punctuated and accentuated by the visible "grinning" of the father, whom the son judges to be "not afraid for my life, either, / As the wild engines stand at my knees." To recognize imminent death—upward in the person of his father, downward in the descent of the son, and all around in the ferocious traffic—is one of the chief lessons of poetry. Except for the somewhat overdone concluding stanza, with an exact repetition of the poem's first line, "The Hospital Window" is a "pin-tingling hand" of a poem. Its life is in its perception and imagination of death, and the grown son here is in control of the meaning of his father's mortal precedent for his own human life.

Drowning with Others: None Shall Survive

"The Hospital Window" sets forth in gentler terms than "The String" or some of the war poems Dickey's preoccupation with survivorship. The idea seems on the surface to be a selfish one, but in fact it turns on the point of the poet's recognition of his part in the human race; he sees and fully comprehends the interrelationship of all people, especially when it comes to mortality. "Drowning with Others" functions for Dickey to pluralize his recurrent ghostly brother-figure.

The elements of water and light are enough to transform the physical appearance, the mass, the weight, of the people involved in swimming for their lives; and the poet himself is led to drifting syntax and mystic-sounding images. Hanging on the edge of willful obscurity, Dickey allows just enough hard detail to seduce us back into the pursuit of the poem's meanings. The figures in the water reach and touch and appear to fly with wingbones of the shoulderblades. The people become participants in the elements: "If I opened my arms, I could hear / / Every shell in the sea find the word / It has tried to put into my mouth." The sea's overwhelming power has translated into the speaker's belief that the sea is trying to communicate. As much as its title suggests a communion of humanity, this poem is actually more self-indulgent, more falsely sensation-seeking, than most of Dickey's more mature works. Like "Into the Stone" for its mysticism and its singular, abstracted vision, "Drowning with Others" might have gone well in Dickey's first book, whose "The Underground Stream" it also recalls. Dickey himself somewhat derogates the poem in *Self-Interviews*: "I wanted to call the book *Drowning with Others,* so I decided I'd better write a poem by the same title to give some status to the book's title. I don't think it's a very strong poem; it seems awfully obscure to me" (*SI,* 116).

Perhaps the strongest case for the poem's value is in its representation of the survivorship theme, with a bizarre turn of mind given by the narrator, who, whether he actually, finally drowns or not, is a survivor for a long enough time that he may tell the experience. Additionally, with the reference to the merging of meaning with the elements of nature, the poet emphasizes his theme from "The Owl King" and elsewhere that *things* have the power to emanate meaning and energy from themselves, not entirely to be the inventions—the fictions—of the human observers, and yet those emanations become incorporated with and help to define the personality of the participants in those experiences.

Part of this survivorship effect is to come to the edge of mortal mergence, to enter a region of potential oblivion and the most intense self-awareness. In "The Lifeguard," the young man who has failed at his job feels guilt which is heightened by his own approximation to death. He has been submerged, with the frenzy of feeling his breath waste away, in the cold, lightless lake where he feels the black mud in his hands. To have failed in his responsibility is one thing, but to have lived instead of his ward, to have been left unable even for that futile cry, "Let me die in his place!" is to multiply the mortal despair. The child comes to the lifeguard alone, after dark, in the moonlight, after all have gone to bed; and even though the lifeguard has for a moment the bright moon-child from the heart of the forest in his arms, the final despair is devastating—the illusion is insistently illusory. Despite all signs of recognition and regeneration, the lifeguard's own survival comes to the terrible futility of water spilling through his helpless fingers. The comfort Dickey sometimes perceives in nature is absent, as in general "The Lifeguard" is less overt in calling for powers to come from nature. The images are more naturally blended in the consciousness of the lifeguard. It is not as though he pursues meanings so much as he is tragically caught by them. The natural images—moon, water, forest, mud, human faces—reinforce and embody the experience he has had during the fateful day.

One consequence of being a survivor is to have perspective upon destruction no one else can have. One of Dickey's most unusual survivor poems is "The Dream Flood," in which the narrator has achieved to such a state of detachment as to gain the perspective of the Deluge, the destroyer of biblical proportions, which gives the poet the occasion to imagine truly overwhelming force. Distance can become, in poems, a dream; thus the poet can reach into his psyche in ways that so-called realism will not allow.

"The Dream Flood" begins with the speaker's invocation, oddly, to "ask and receive / The secret of falling unharmed / Forty nights from the darkness of Heaven." Conspicuously, Dickey alludes to the forty days' rain of Noah's Flood, but he also (perhaps unwittingly) calls to mind the fall of the angels. The poem, being a "dream flood" by designation, sets about immediately to dislocate somewhat surrealistically the actual cosmography: "descend to the moon / Where it lies on the ground." Dickey, of course, is using a phenomenon he often employs, the appearance of the moon in some reflecting surface, usually, and in this case, in water. Earlier, in the first poem of *Drowning with Others,* "The Lifeguard," Dickey uses the floating moon as a prefiguration of the lifeguard's imagined ability to walk on the water. In "The Dream Flood," the reality of the moon's light, as it is indeed "sunlight transmitted by stone," is eerily accurate even as it sets our reason on edge—but no more than the concept of world-wide flood would do. Once on the earth, however, the rainwaters (now personified and accommodated with poetic intelligence) move more realistically, building and seeping with mind-boggling dimensions, but without the arch diversion of sense and common sense that the poet practices upon us in the first two stanzas.

Dickey's skillful selectivity in the catastrophe—he talks repetitively of the horses and trees—allows the readers to supply to such understatement their own intensity for the truest comprehension of disaster. The dream-like floating of things is as eerie as the moon's inversion. The horses float contained in their stalls: "Their bodies in cell blocks of wood / Hang like a dust that has taken / Their shape without knowing of horses."

Later, the Flood-Poet says, "I withdraw, in feeling the cloud / Of Heaven call dazzlingly to me / To drop off my horses and forests," and the poem turns its attention from "grasses and fence wire of glory / That have burned together like a coral with depth" to the effect of the Flood upon human beings. But the Flood recalls only women, no men, as its victim-lovers—no surprise, after closely reading "The Enclosure." When the last three stanzas lean so heavily upon the female victims, the reader is justifiably driven back to see that the rain, flood, and sun images are standard images of maleness, of the dominating, fructifying principles that can turn destructive, as Coleridge's Ancient Mariner testifies. The male principle is almost omnipotent, until the time comes at the end to bring life again to the dead. The poem conveys an immense sadness at such paradox, and one wonders why Dickey chose to exclude this imperfect but affecting poem from *Poems 1957–1967*. The Flood-Poet is called "impotent waters," and the evaporating "sunlight / Straining in vain / With her lost, dead weight" cannot restore life. The last line ("Lift. I am dreaming. Lift.") is what each woman "shall implore," but the chief impact of this dream flood is one of more general destruction for the world and terrible enlightenment for the Flood-Poet, who is the ultimate survivor, the destroyer of all things besides itself.

Art, and the Body in the Grasp of the World

While "The Dream Flood" represents an extreme effort by the poet to distance himself from the physical action of his poem, "The Scratch" drives the poet back into the body. But, like "The War Wound" (1964) and earlier war poems, it functions as an emblem. The poet speculates that the scratch on his wrist was "once hid in a fiery twist / Of brier," evoking the theme of potentiality seen in "The Owl King." But intellect dominates the poem, not the thing-ness of things: "I watchfully sit down / to lift it wisely, and see / Blood come, as at play." The intellectual speculation does not allow us to accept passionately the Victorian resolve and quasi-heroic posture at the end: "I shall dream of a crown till I do."

For all its aesthetic straining, "The Scratch" reiterates Dickey's interest in beginning his poems with images that stick in the mind. His poem-making generally proceeds directly out of the things of the natural world. "A Birth" shows how the poet makes life within his own imagination and then gives it free rein. Art is thus an illusion in the service of perceiving the most independent, vital conditions, the most natural: "Inventing a story with grass," says Dickey, "I find a young horse deep inside it."

With its particular attention to mother and child, "A Birth" signifies the creation of things in art which then generate other, seemingly independent things—like one's own children. The four-stanza poem breaks cleanly midway, with the narrator's contemplation of his "inventing a story" in the first half; and, his "mind freed of its own creature," he turns "to find [himself] deep in [his] life." The interlocking of life-forces and art is directly reminiscent of "A Dog Sleeping on My Feet" and "Trees and Cattle," as well as the family-conscious poems of *Into the Stone*. "A Birth" clearly identifies the poet as the central figure, not the other subjects (or objects) in it. The poet is, of course, in charge of the poem—the whole thing is an act of his imagination. But within the third stanza, the language is notably passive (in fact, it is relatively passive from line two, after "Inventing a story"). The speaker's creative effort immediately gives way to the story's own almost magical volition: "I find a young horse deep inside it." The second stanza begins, "And he is free, strangely, without me," so the poet's story turns over to become "his story"—the horse's—which then melds with the sun in the story. At the end, when the poet has presumably returned to his own real world, with his child and his mother in the room, the return of the real-world sun generates yet another horse, another story.

The affirmation of art in the poem is that it has a reality that lies beyond the conscious control of the artist. The imagination is able to construct images and stories that take off in whatever direction they "naturally" go, rather than following some line that the artist feels he may absolutely manipulate. "A Birth" begins as a pastoral emblem-poem, but it begins to breathe without the conscious volition of the poet. As is often the case in later Dickey poems, the landscape is taken over, given vitality, specifically by an animal. Dickey does not normally write poems about art—his best aesthetic statements are in his poems as poems and in his prose criticism—but these earlier works of aesthetic intention do foreshadow such extensive explorations of the subject as "The Eye-Beaters" and *The Zodiac*.

"In the Lupanar at Pompeii" is made with style and diction more like later Dickey poems (or like those early exceptions, "The Performance" and "The Hospital Window"), with their force of simple declarative sentences, without, for the most part, poetical rhetoric and sententiousness. The tourist-poet is loose among the ruins of a glorious past civilization, seeking significance and longing for some universality by virtue of the references to other cultures in other, faraway places. But here Dickey has elected to write about the destruction of Pompeii from the point of view of a man who wants mainly to know about the ancient whorehouses.

The poem's specific lesson, however, given out of the mouths of the "painted, unchanging women" and those of "the desperate dead," is "Passion. Before we die / Let us hope for no longer / But truly know it." The lesson is easily said, and one receives it with a touch of humor; but, as with "Beauty is truth, truth beauty," told by Keats's Grecian Urn, a suspect orator, the final utterance of Dickey's poem is equally suspect, with the dusty, incinerated dead, mouthing of passion, where theirs was found in the heat of their deaths, more than in the carnal heat of whores.

Perhaps the strongest section of the poem is in Dickey's statement about the nature of lust:

> I think of the marvel of lust
> Which can always, at any moment,
> Become more than it believed,
> And almost always is less:
> I think of its possible passing
> Beyond, into tender awareness,
> Into helplessness, weeping, and death:
> It must be like the first
> Soft floating of ash. . . .

Almost nowhere until he gets to "Sun" and "Adultery," both in the "Falling" section of *Poems 1957–1967,* does Dickey touch so sensitively upon the frayed nerves of human sexuality.

"In the Lupanar at Pompeii" is a good poem but not a great one. It combines Dickey's emblematic technique, taking the figures fixed in stone to devise meaning from them, as well as from Dickey's continuing interest in the ghostly dead. Here, though, the dead are less truly immanent. They function as mere voices of the petrified emblems; their passion is only wispily evoked, and the poet himself is left as a half-humorous, mildly nervous man intelligent enough to take the serious occasion of Pompeii to think on things as important as lust and death. Like "Ode on a Grecian Urn," it reminds us of the terrible gap between the dead and their stony immortality in art.

"Snow on a Southern State" is another of those poems that begins with physical dislocation, with the poet purposefully disrupting the readers' expectations of geography, balance, and direction. Using the word "labor" to indicate in the first line how his effort is conscious, the poet describes his movement on a train. The sense of reflection, the ghostlike apprehension of himself as some floating creature outside the self, the feeling of odd directions and inverted expectations, all contribute to the poem's efforts to create the otherworldliness so often conjured up by snowfall. The alteration and concealment of familiar physical forms, the muffling of sounds, the tactile gray of the cold snowy days help the poet bring his narrator to new insights about himself and the world around him. The poignancy of one's return to home country is more to be adjusted for the speaker's coming to unfamiliar sights now that the snow, so infrequent in the South, is visiting at the same time. In a manner recalling "A Screened Porch in the

Country," the chief early impact of the snow leads the narrator "dumbly" to address the denizens outside the train beyond his voice, to tell them comfortingly of the snow's transience, that it is clearly passing, as he is, through their town like a harmless ghost of themselves.

The most peculiar effect of the snow comes later to the speaker. As memory alters the past and thus renews it, this snow alters the place, all its sensuousness, and obscures but also renews its covered land for the narrator. The poem turns in its later stanzas to speak ominously of "weddings opposed by the world," "A dead cotton field," and "the equilibrium / Of bones . . . falling, falling." Such retreat into vague, even obscurantist, incidents, away from the long, relatively secure description of the scene, somewhat dislocated but secure, is perhaps too much for the poem to bear. Mostly it suggests the power of the mind in art to alter the past and the present, as snow can alter even the familiar scenes of our homes.

As Dickey's effort to deal in poems about the poetic enterprise may be seen to dwindle away (neither "Snow on a Southern State" nor "To Landrum Guy, Beginning to Write at Sixty" saw publication before *Drowning with Others,* and Dickey omitted both from *Poems 1957–1967*), it is exciting to look once again at "A Dog Sleeping on My Feet," which follows as though the poet has burst out to acknowledge what he so intensely held within himself in "Listening to Foxhounds." He abandons the consideration of the group's judgment upon a man who would imagine himself in union with the quarry—the fox. He openly writes of himself as a writer, in close physical contact with his dog, who in turn has been dreaming (the poet imagines) of chasing the fox.

The poem strains somewhat in lines that discourse upon the problem of verbalizing natural, spiritual experiences:

> . . . my hand, which speaks in a daze
> The hypnotized language of beasts,
> Shall falter, and fail
>
> Back into the human tongue. . . .

But it is a plain statement of Dickey's view that the truest power of language is sensual and the truest source of inspiration is a physical apprehension of nature. The poem ends with a return to reality, wife and sons: "From the dream of an animal." Like Frost's "Stopping by Woods on a Snowy Evening," Dickey's poem resumes the world of social necessity

("Assembling the self I must wake to") with all the residue he can sustain of "the scent of the fox" upon his waking. He must sleep "to grow back [his] legs," to return fully to the human world; but there is a certain amount of duplicity in the poet's speaking throughout as a poet, a writer who is conscious of using his material. Nonetheless, it is instructive as to Dickey's attitudes toward nature and art. It reemphasizes the importance to Dickey's art of animals—dog and fox—as the best guides to human participation in nature.

Animate Creatures—Signs

It is unusual for Dickey to conclude in so palpably didactic a manner as the final three lines of "The Movement of Fish": "One must think of this to understand / The instinct of fear and trembling, / And, of its one movement, the depth." In a direct line of fish-in-the-stream images from Faulkner and Hemingway, Dickey displays a minor turn of Kierkegaardian existentialism. The image is memorable, if not entirely original, and the poem begins with a startlingly simple truth: "No water is still, on top. / Without wind, even, it is full / Of a chill, superficial agitation." Dickey equates, one supposes, the surface of everyday human things with "The trivial, quivering / Surface," under which the fish have True Being. The implications are (1) that the human being who makes his feeble breaths and sounds, barely rippling the water, is not in touch with the profundity of the waters or of the fish's experience; (2) that fish are instinctually attuned since they are literally immersed in the medium of their sustenance; (3) that fish are threatened from above (the people in boats) and from below (whatever fatal pursuers are out of sight in the dark depths), a nameless threat that is also connected, at least for the poet, with the fact that fish swim suddenly, as in terror, "picking up speed, still shooting / / Through half-gold, / Going nowhere." The emptiness of that observation is most unusual in Dickey's work, as it implies that nothing really can be done to save our souls. Tragic experience is deep, but mere survival is of dubious value since meaning and direction are left void at the end of this poem. Such starkness in Dickey's poems, as rarely as it occurs, stands as a challenge to the discovery of meaning in the simple vitality of living things.

Richard Howard has said of *Drowning with Others*, "James Dickey is still a poet of process rather than of particular presences, and of presences rather than persons, in his apprehension of nature as of selfhood."[1] Surely one of

Dickey's finest poems is "The Heaven of Animals," a work that glorifies process and, at the same time, as Howard calls it, "pure recurrence."[2]

"The Heaven of Animals" resembles "The Performance" in its clean, persuasive narrative line, as though pure description is not the real point. Temporal flow in the timeless setting of heaven is the paradoxical focus of our experience through the poem. "The Performance" echoes again in the depiction of stoic necessity relieved by an oddly unexpected joy, a curious sense of ecstasy in the midst of sanctioned carnage. The carnage is necessary in this Heaven; it is the course of heavenly order. But there is also relief that one might feel in knowing—absolutely knowing—what one's role is, even if one is the victim. It is the animal world's version of Plato's Republic, in which justice is defined as each man's doing his job. The astonishment of the animals is emphasized, perhaps to avoid suspicion of their being bored with eternal certainty: ". . . claws and teeth grown perfect, / More deadly than they can believe." (It is like lust in Pompeii.)

The poet seems to want heaven's perfection to extend to all the animals, but his own sympathies—his best satisfactions—lie clearly with the predators (who are not themselves portrayed as prey of other predators). The passive prey are "fulfilling themselves without pain," but "They tremble." The poet's effort to make a heaven of (for?) animals is not nearly so democratic as it may at first appear. The pleasantest of all worlds is one in which the strong have willing (and trembling) prey; it is the fulfillment of the predator's sadistic desire for fear in his quarry that we see most of. The poem is about the perfection of the law of the jungle, without the horrid cycle at its fullest—no vultures to rip away the flesh of lions and leopards. That would be too disquieting for a poet who seizes the opportunity to make a world in which the strong prevail without guilt, without compunction, only to savor joy and flight, the savagery of killing without the obligations of consequence.

Such a poem would not be possible without a fallen world; as Richard Howard says, "when this world is called a fallen world, what is meant is that our soul, our aspirations, our hungers have collapsed into our present body, our present landscape, and that the instruments of our tran-scendence are at the same time the tools of undoing: *resurrection for a little while,* as Dickey laments and exults."[3] Survivorship subsides as a theme, for here all survive. if that is the ultimate goal. But what of the emptiness of purpose? The prospect of heaven is shaky enough in terms of Dickey's poems; such perfect order and conditions are beyond comprehension, even aspiration, in such poems as "The Performance," "The Owl King,"

"Dover: Believing in Kings," and, later, "The Eye-Beaters," "May Day Sermon," and *The Zodiac.* "The Heaven of Animals" is a chilling poem, however perfected and articulated; it is of a world entirely different from the humane vision of "The Sheep Child" or "Madness," in which the poet writes of animal aberrations but has not abandoned his basic compassion for some cold dream of domination.

Perhaps the fixed and predictable carnage of "The Heaven of Animals" is one way of Dickey's handling metaphysically based fear. Earlier in his life, prior to the influence of his Vanderbilt University astronomy professor, Carl Siefert, Dickey "had always been like Pascal, frightened by the silence of the infinite spaces" (*SI,* 37). But later, as a poet, his fears in nature are most often when animals are present or are thought to be. With "Fog Envelops the Animals" fear is a major emotion, especially as it is unmanageable, unaccountably exuded as a vibration or overtone of the natural world as a whole. In this respect, the poem is like "The Shark's Parlor," "Pursuit from Under," and other late Dickey poems. The imagery associated with fog is also something that recurs later, particularly in "May Day Sermon." However, the fear Dickey's narrators feel has less to do with the fog than with what might come or go in it. No doubt the fog-enshrouded creatures are symbolic of some more fearful thing—death itself, probably—but the beasts are there, waiting as images of the dreadful abstraction. (It is in this aspect that, once again, "The Heaven of Animals" proves the exception. Heaven is where death and sensation are present but fear is not. However much the prey may tremble, oblivion is abjured, and fear is therefore abated.) To the narrator of "Fog Envelops the Animals," the fog is not only a monolithic threat, but he also personifies it at the same time as he discriminates among his own "selves": "Soundlessly whiteness is eating / My visible self alive." Then the speaker moves suppositiously into some version of foggish ecstasy:

> I shall enter this world like the dead,
> Floating through tree trunks on currents
> And streams of untouchable pureness
>
> That shine without thinking of light.

Even as he takes on qualities of the fog, he comes to feel that some of those were originally his: "I feel my own long-hidden, / Long-sought invisibility / Come forth from my solid body."

Man the Precarious Intruder—Transcendence Desired

"Fog Envelops the Animals" deals with an important poetic act for
Dickey—not the same as an aesthetic act—that is, the assimilation of
some profound emotional insight by willfully imagining oneself in extraordinary relation with the ordinary. The speaker of this poem is
present—the hunter—and he is actively imagining the experience of
being foglike. For instance, he not only envelops animals; he also pene-
trates and interfuses with trees: "Floating through tree trunks" and
"Through the hearts of the curdling oak trees." It is this additional aspect
of transcendence at which Dickey is boldest, and perhaps most vulnerable:
". . . I don't think you can get to sublimity without courting the
ridiculous. Therefore, a good many of my poems deal with farfetched
situations. . . . [Critics] give you the impression that we belong to a
generation whose catch-word is 'Aw, come off it! You don't really feel
anything like that!' I don't want to come off it! I want to go *with* it! . . . I
think that cynicism is probably the easiest, least profitable, and least
valuable human emotion. . . . I'm a born believer and not a disbeliever.
This doubtless has its dangers. But such as it is, there it is" (*SI,* 65–66).
He is willing to accept the insights of the human creature who has
imagined himself one with nature, and then he improves on nature. He
reapplies the human ability to imagine and experience vicariously things
that no one, no creature human or nonhuman, has ever experienced, thus
probing further the limits of the human mind and body.

More specifically, by imagining the extraordinary condition, by this
stretching the limits of conscious human experience, Dickey is able to
probe—as poets should, as great poets do—the areas of human experience
laid over by familiarity or dullness or timidity. Especially as Dickey
reaches deep to examine fear, as in "Fog Envelops the Animals," do we find
him most pressurized, most persuasive, not, as with many other poets,
when he is faced with tragic circumstances, with pity. Dickey responds to
terror. The Melvillean strain of "Silence. Whiteness. Hunting," with
which Dickey ends this poem, is homiletic only in its paraphrase. For the
poet, it is experiential. In his best poems, the reader is also allowed. It is
mythic activity, to reimagine the world in terms that move humankind
even without their quite knowing why. And the process is infinitely
variable: "If sensations turn into soul—into an ineffable quality that can
never be accounted for by the sensations themselves—it is because the
sensations reach an ever-changing mind that transforms them, as a merely
passive receiver, the sort of mind Locke likens to blank paper, could not."[4]

Sometimes the action of the mind upon nature is morally unsettling, as in "The Summons," in which the narrator raises a call which is truly evil. Unlike "The Call," of *Into the Stone,* which is made by a desperate father who seeks his son lost in the woods, "The Summons" presents a speaker who is almost morally condescending to himself. There are even signs that the speaker is deceiving himself. At the very outset he says, "For something out of sight, / I cup a grass-blade in my hands, / Tasting the root, and blow." It seems obvious, although at least three other times the poet speaks too generally of the "beast" he hunts ("some being," "something"), that the true-life hunter would certainly know what beast he called and what sort of fairly specific response to expect. What is most curious, and most directly incriminating, is that the hunter uses a love-call to draw the beast to death at the same time as he tries to preempt moral censure by alluding to his lost innocence as the poem closes:

> . . . I pluck my longbow off the limb
> Where it shines with a musical light,
> And crouch within death, awaiting
> The beast in water, in love
> With the palest and gentlest of children,
> Whom the years have turned deadly with knowledge:
> Who summons him forth, and now
> Pulls wide the great, thoughtful arrow.

The duplicity of the act, of the quarry's being enticed by a self-consciously ironic human being, is emphasized by the self-satisfied coldness of the hunter's "great, thoughtful arrow." It is prefigurative of "The Firebombing," in which the aesthetic distance of a bomber-pilot allows him to feel both aware and absolved. Even though the word "beast" is used to denominate the hunter's target, not enough can be done to exonerate the poet for his "summons" to death of the natural creature who seeks love. Whereas "Fog Envelops the Animals" insists upon the presence of fear as a crucial ingredient to meaningful hunting, this poem is entirely fearless—a strike from ambush—entirely invulnerable to the compassionating influences of nature, entirely demonstrative of the poet whose human reason has allowed him to seduce and kill with impunity some grand beast who comes to the call of love. Unlike the kind of love Dickey shows in "Madness" (1969), whose frenetic passion also leads to death, there is no threat here to the hunter, no true participation or identification.

A similar distance from nature is evident in "For the Nightly Ascent of the Hunter Orion Over a Forest Clearing," which foreshadows *The Zodiac* and raises the question of why Dickey is so taken with the far-distant constellations. He has been a pilot-navigator in wartime, and he has studied astronomy as a college student and as an amateur astronomer; but it seems especially pertinent that these constellations, as they are named for earth-forms, imaginings of poets and artists, stand as projections outward of the human intellect and imagination.

"For the Nightly Ascent" ends with the speaker, after "ambiguous undulations" (to crib from Wallace Stevens's "Sunday Morning"), finding himself somehow not only a mortal hunter who might want to be a tree even as he wants stealthy mobility, but also "a man of stars." In the final lines a paradox emerges. Dickey's narrator has consciously sought the cosmic, unconscious knowledge of the heavens. Granted, the transformation of the mortal man into the starry Orion is only by analogy ("Unless he rises / / As does the hunter Orion"), but the effort is real. The man is aware that he stands with one foot "longing to tiptoe / And the other to take the live / Stand of a tree that belongs here." In some ways it recalls the curious mixture of vegetation and animal-spirits in "The Other," or the beast and angel figures in "To His Children in Darkness," but this poem signals an even more expansive Dickey aspiration, to contact and to use the powers of infinite, starry space.

Dickey's transcendent leap in this poem, however, does not allow him to fly utterly away. The speaker begins, "Now secretness dies of the open," and the reader recalls those occasional experiences of openness and exaltation from which the closed-off human creature more often than not has prevented himself. But this poem is strange in its human-nonhuman straddling; the beasts and birds of the night awaken, gain power from their various nocturnal sources—"the owl's gaze / / Most slowly begins to create / Its sight from the death of the sun"; the mouse is invigorated by knowing of the owl; and the fox comes out of the ground as though recharged by earth's magnetism or something equally vibrant—and the speaker, moving through the creaturely activity, emerges into openness and then aspires upward, away from the magnetic living in which he is immersed. The paradox is extended as Orion (and the man, one presumes) is illuminated by his own self-light, perhaps as each night creature has its own special illumination and source of vitality (as "The Owl King" also depicts). In "Fog Envelops the Animals" the speaker's invisibility comes from within to help him identify with the fog: in "For the Nightly Ascent" what is left *behind* is invisibility, and what is come to is "the light / Of himself."

In "The Rib," Dickey alludes slightly to Adam and Eve, as one might anticipate from the title, but mainly the poet uses his own body as meaningful object, as emblem, through which he may perceive and empower himself anew. Somewhat as he does in "The Summons," Dickey begins with an effort to mystify by using the general "Something." The mysterious thing in this case is quickly shown to be the decayed carcass of an indistinguishable animal. Dickey captures squarely the feeling of threat which surrounds such discoveries (survivorship may sometimes result in sudden paranoia): a casual walker never knows exactly how such deaths happened, if the bones are the only remains. Then the person may well grow apprehensive that the unknown killer—be it disease, enemy, or simply amorphous death—still lurks about. The rib in hand causes the speaker to attribute death to all his surroundings.

As the hunter contemplates "the wounds of beasts," he is forced to consider his own fleshly package of mortality: "A rib in my right side speaks / To me more softly / / Than Eve. . . ." This reaching into the self because of having touched some external emblem is reminiscent of the poems in *Into the Stone,* especially the "War" section, but the embodiment of the narrator's mortal condition into himself is more persuasive than the lurking presence of the dead brother in "The Underground Stream" and other poems.

Unhappily, "The Rib" suffers from weak language and a trite-sounding ending: "I rise, going moonward toward better / And better sleep." But Dickey's decision to exclude "The Rib" from *Poems 1957–1967* seems less defensible than most of his other such decisions. The most justifiable reason may be that a reversion to "love" as a purportedly major part of the poem, after only one casual reference to Eve in the final three stanzas, suggests that Dickey is trying for more universal significance than this poem will bear. Perhaps more interestingly, this poem speaks of a conjunction of violence and love which comes to have more emphasis as Dickey's career progresses.

However much Dickey strives for transcendent experience in them, emblematic poems such as "The Rib" allow him to get in and out of meanings with minimal emotional stress; they stand ultimately as clever foci of considerations. Sometimes the poet's efforts at empowering vision extend to images of his family. "A Screened Porch in the Country" stands more daringly on the edge of family and nature, waiting there for glowing insights, if not sparks to fly. It is notable for the poet's detachment from the objects—family, in this case—of his contemplation, a detachment

similar to that in "The Hospital Window" and "The Celebration," also
family poems.

When Dickey describes the people on the porch by calling them "bodies
softening to shadow," he summons the reader to accept something of what
Conrad meant when he wrote in *Heart of Darkness* that, to Marlow, "the
meaning of an episode was not inside like a kernel but outside, enveloping
the tale which brought it out only as a glow brings out a haze, in the
likeness of one of these misty halos that sometimes are made visible by the
spectral illumination of moonshine."[5] Dickey's people are seen only as
projections of themselves, their own shadows from their lamplike house:

> . . . until
> They come to rest out in the yard
> In a kind of blurred golden country
> In which they more deeply lie
> Than if they were being created
> Of Heavenly light.

The distinction that Dickey makes is important, for in most of his poems,
it is clear that human beings are superior. Here, though, he elevates some
nonspecific, nonrational essence of the people to absolute prominence. The
second stanza explicitly relegates "The smallest creatures"—animals—to
unconsciousness, or at least wordlessness, although their own essence is
somehow accessible to the poet, if not to the people on the porch. In this
aspect—the primacy of the poetic act—this poem is like "Listening to
Foxhounds." Dickey allows to these mysterious edge-of-night-light creatures the experience of music: "Sing, if they can, / Or, if they can't, simply
shine . . . , / Pulsating and thinking of music." The claim for humanity,
though, is that it can

> . . . become
> More than human, and enter the place
> Of small, blindly singing things,
> Seeming to rejoice
> Perpetually, without effort,
> Without knowing why
> Or how they do it.

The natural creatures are fine, and people are fine; but the best is when
people turn almost passive, "Emitted by their own house," projected into

nature by their very humanness. The poem is notably romantic in its depiction of the excellence of nonrational knowledge, the highway to transcendence it provides. But Dickey's firm hold on physical reality, the actual scene, allows the reader to stop short of the loosest, flabbiest magico-mystical qualities of such poetry. Perhaps the deftest touch is that Dickey draws up the reins of supposition right at the end of the poem: "Seeming to rejoice," only "seeming," he says. The human encounter with nonhuman nature must always be slightly suspect, slightly tenuous, for the connection is always susceptible to peculiarly human rationality and imagination.

"The Change" reiterates Dickey's interest in the primordial essence of all natural things, thus the essence of humanity. Here he finds it in a hammerhead shark, a brother who can never evolve, as the poet says, "No millions of years shall yet turn him / / From himself to a man in love." Yet the poet finds in the creature the living spark that has somehow persisted and produced humankind over those same eons. The poet speculates what he would be if he could somehow embody both the shark and the person, to become

> . . . what I would make of myself
> In ten millions years, if I could,
>
> And arise from my brute of a body
> To a thing the world never thought of
> In a place as apparent as Heaven.

This poet's pursuit is for something at "the heart of [his] brain," not to discount what the human intellect perceives and constructs, but to include with those powers something of the brute force and the instinctual knowing of creatures so mysteriously long-existing as the shark.

"The Change" also recalls more obliquely the theme of brotherhood, the unknown companion of Dickey's youth and of his prebirth. The sense of brotherhood that Dickey feels with the natural world, especially with beasts of prey, is tied intimately with his sense of survivorship in a predominantly hostile universe, a place in which such a brotherhood and such combinations of power as he aspires to in this poem are the prerequisites for immortality.

Nonetheless, in the searching for transcendent power, as risky as it may be, the poet does not forget the needs of beauty and gentleness, the fine perceptions and creations of people:

> . . . the heart of my brain has spoken . . .
> Gently of ends and beginnings,
> Gently of sources and outcomes,
> Impossible, brighter than sunlight.

The words of the poet have been subsumed in the radiant knowledge of suprarational powers of insight, of ways to know that only the universe as a whole may possess but which Dickey desires. The shark is to remain one of his most potent images of essence, most conspicuously in "The Shark's Parlor" (1965). Ironically, as he calls the poem "The Change," Dickey's overwhelming sense of the unchangingness of the shark over the centuries is the major source of interest of the poem. It is only his speculation, his wild imaginative flight, not even very convincing, that suggests that any change is possible in people, much less in the shark.

In most of his poems, though, Dickey believes firmly in the efficacy of thinking, in the power of the human imagination to penetrate the physical world to perceive and even to affect the spiritual world, even to affect the creatures of the nonhuman natural world. In "Autumn" the poet infers that trees somehow tune into the capacity of human beings, that they may think themselves through the fall changes, to turn leaves, perhaps, then, even to prepare for their own mortal conclusions: "I see the tree think it will turn / Brown, and tomorrow at dawn / It will change as it thinks it will change."

The subtlety of Dickey's poem goes beyond easy personification. The poet observes that the changes will come faster than the trees believe; even as human beings, even those who become aware of their mortality, always come to death sooner than they know and almost certainly sooner than they wish. The trees come to their deaths, their falls, as they recall the glorious greens of their fruitful time, just as a dying man may recall something of his own rich life.

The apparition of an angel allows the poet cheaply to reestablish the religious concerns that run throughout the poem, but it also raises doubts about the integrity of the poet's vision, as though he changes key and departs his original nature imagery as the burden of his song.

The last poem in the book, "In the Mountain Tent," allows the narrator access to both animate and inanimate nature. He gives in to the "profound, unspeakable law" which then allows him the state of mind which admits him into the natural arena, the world of the essences of things, the world of the truest light on nature, the best insights of human and nonhuman nature. The spirit of creation appears to be intelligent and purposeful, as Dickey describes the "thought-out leaves of the wood," suggesting that the leaves are the manifestations of the thought-creation of trees and ultimately of some spirit-force behind and beyond them. The minds of animals, then, become the ground for the poet's contemplations, the power source as well as the subject matter of his spiritual exercises. And the ultimate word for the man seems to be poetry which emerges as though from the mind and quality of nature's creatures, not something that could merely be manufactured by the rational, distilled creature— man: "I am there like the dead, or the beast / Itself, which thinks of a poem." But a poem is a made thing, the creation-again of the spirit of the natural world:

Czeslaw Milosz, the 1980 Nobel laureate, writes in "Ars Poetica?"—

. . . poetry is rightly said to be dictated by a daimonion,
though it's an exaggeration to maintain that he must be an angel . . .
. . . poems should be written rarely and reluctantly,
under unbearable duress and only with the hope
that good spirits, not evil ones, choose us for their instruments.[6]

Dickey's American rather than East European mentality, buoyed with some senseless optimism in a hard world, almost invariably leads him to believe that no matter what comes as poetry, the spirit must be good. He does not seem so much to screen out as to expect that to let oneself have "free-falling" access to the minds of the beasts is to have access to the immanent spirit of creation and therefore of good—not evil—daimonions.

It is fitting that the last poem in Dickey's second book so wholly and enthusiastically embrace the natural world and exclaim its present right of poetry, but one must remember that the voice of the poet here is only as mediator: "From holes in the ground comes my voice / In the God-silenced tongue of the beasts. / 'I shall rise from the dead,' I am saying." These last lines recall "To His Children in Darkness," in which the poet sees himself in forms both beastly and angelic, his voice somehow miraculous, in dreamlike authority, to tell the truths of the human soul by synthesizing (in that earlier case, for his sons) the forces of the natural and supranatural world as it comes to glory in a human being's self-consciousness and his ability to be conscious of the external world as well. It is a risky, threatening business, this transcendence. We must be bold.

Chapter Four

The Middle Phase, and Glory

Helmets (1964)

In *Self-Interviews,* Dickey says that *"Helmets* was an attempt to deepen some of the themes that I had announced in *Into the Stone,* but mainly in *Drowning with Others.* The hunting theme took on a much greater importance, and I wanted to get back to the war theme in a way which had nothing to do with flying. . . . I wrote about the war from the standpoint of the infantry where you have a much closer intimacy with what happens to the *people* in a war" *(SI,* 124). Despite the author's statement that hunting is a major theme, however, only "Springer Mountain" is about hunting as one usually understands that term—deer-hunting, in this case. Two other poems apply only slightly. "Winter Trout" is about shooting fish with bow and arrow, and "Approaching Prayer" is an imaginary hunt, from the perspective of a son rummaging through his father's attic, who puts on the head of a boar and imagines being the quarry. As Dickey indicates, *Helmets* does generally avoid the coolness of the earlier "emblem" war poems; it is more down-to-earth since the poems are not about airmen. But there are only three war poems in the book—all good, to be sure, but only three. Perhaps a better way to speak of themes in *Helmets* would be to call hunting and war the *subject matter* of some notable poems: the real *themes* are otherwise. Among them are several variations on the theme of transcendence.

Epiphany: Transcendence through the Single, Startling Image. The first three poems in *Helmets* are visions of transcendence that have virtually nothing to do with hunting or war. They recall certain mystic-insight poems of *Into the Stone,* like "Trees and Cattle" or "Walking on Water," but these in *Helmets* proceed with rhythmic confidence and strainless image-making that mark them as pieces by a truly mature artist. They are tightly contained, visionary, intensely clear, almost surreal poems. "The Dusk of Horses," "Fence Wire," and "At Darien Bridge" are

54

poems whose initial impulse is an image of striking clarity which then develops (like the horse in "A Birth") into a self-sustaining vision which appears to surprise and illuminate even the poet himself.

"The Dusk of Horses" has an omniscient narrator who tells of the puzzlement of horses whose world alters dramatically by the shifting twilight, but without their understanding: "Right under their noses, the green / Of the field is paling away / Because of something fallen from the sky." As he projects his own knowledge to his readers (over his overhearers), the narrator only gradually—like the dusk itself—turns the senses around, shifts the ground of their perception, and finally leads his poem home. The remarkable accomplishment is for Dickey to have given and taken away so much, so many times, in so short a poem. He calls the sun "something fallen from the sky" to establish the ignorance of the horses. He says in the second stanza that they "put down / Their long heads deeper in grass / That only just escapes reflecting them / / As the dream of a millpond would," to draw his simile-recognizing human reader to his aesthetic complicity. And then he proceeds to speak declaratively as though all together—people and horses—are believing in the newly made physical world of this transcendent dusk: "Now they are feeding on solid / Cloud. . . ." As Dickey often does, in such poems as "The Owl King" and "A Screened Porch in the Country," here he explicitly sets human comprehension at a level superior to that of the animals whose image has triggered the poem:

> No beast ever lived who understood
>
> What happened among the sun's fields,
> Or cared why the color of grass
> Fled over the hill while he stumbled. . . .

Thus, transcendence belongs solely to human beings, who can see and rationalize the visions which fall upon them like sudden rains, so that at the end of this poem, readers join in the synthesis of Dickey's narration, whether it be told through the imagined mind of a horse or of an omniscient poet:

> . . . the way to sleep
>
> In a cloud, or in a risen lake,
> Is to walk as though he were still
> In the drained field standing, head down,

> To pretend to sleep when led,
> And thus to go under the ancient white
> Of the meadow, as green goes
>
> And whiteness comes up through his face
> Holding stars and rotten rafters,
> Quiet, fragrant, and relieved.

"Fence Wire" and "At Darien Bridge" are different in that they deal entirely with the human consciousness—no projection into what the flora or fauna may perceive—as it enlightens itself by the sensual imagination.

Transcendence through Purposeful Communion with Nature. "On the Coosawattee"—whose three parts, "By Canoe Through the Fir Forest," "Below Ellijay," and "The Inundation" (all published separately in 1962), depict an excursion foreshadowing the more idyllic sections of *Deliverance*—represents another kind of transcendence, in which the narrator rather self-consciously communes with nature:

> The stones beneath us grow rounder
> As I taste the fretted light fall
> Through living needles to be here
> Like a word I can feed on forever
>
> Or believe like a vision I have
> Or want to conceive out of greenness.

His willful insights are shared with a canoeing companion, Braselton, who remains unnamed until Part III, when the canoe overturns in rough water and the two spent paddlers are found by "Lucas Gentry and his hunting dog." The narrator's vision of the man-made lake rising to subsume the Coosawattee River, where he and Braselton almost die, is profoundly affected by the Miltonic "Genius of the shore,"[1] Lucas Gentry, "Who may have been the accepting spirit of the place / Come to call us to higher ground." With such a mysterious guardian hovering, the poet seems to recall with more kindly memory the ghostly figures of earlier poems, thus attaining a transcendence that the less mature Dickey, with his unreasonably guilty apprehension of the guardian spirits, might have missed. The furor of the rushing water subsides as the new lake rises over its rocks and gorges, but the canoers are left to remember and, presumably, to hold their lives more precious than before because of that memory.

Two other poems, "Winter Trout" and "In the Marble Quarry," also narrate transcendent experiences in which the poet seems to be consciously seeking enlightenment. "Winter Trout" recalls both "The Dusk of Horses" ("In the concrete cells of the hatchery / He nourished a dream of living / Under the ice") and "The Movement of Fish" ("A pure void of shadowy purpose / Where the gods live, attuning the world"), poems in which the narrator always appears less astonished at his new insights than gratified that his expectations of profundity are fulfilled.

Sometimes Dickey's urgency is unseemly as he pursues the transcendent Other, something mysterious associated, but not always identical, with the immanent spirit in nature that Dickey "announced" in his first two books. Few of his works press harder for transcendence than "Springer Mountain," and few have had more bare-faced publicity from the poet himself. Dickey quotes the entire poem in *Self-Interviews,* after saying, "*I* never took off my clothes and entered into a ritual dance with the animal I'd been trying to kill. *I* never did anything like this, but I aspire to it" (*SI,* 126).

Woods are often a place of ecstasy in Dickey's work, but not exactly joyous, and not exactly Dante's dark night of the soul, either. Rather, they are the place where a modern man can rediscover his natural self. For Dickey, man's genesis was in the primeval forest, not in the slime and sea of Tennyson or in the marsh and mire which spawn the "minimal" life forms of Theodore Roethke's primordial world. It is as though Dickey thinks of man as a species that found itself—who identified himself—when he became a hunter (actually rather late on the evolutionary clock). Dickey's narrator in "Springer Mountain" chases naked after a deer through the winter woods to "ritualize" his natural self.

Despite its several flaws, this poem does manage to say that the "middle-aged, softening" hunter's experience of primal nature is almost as much the result of his running heedlessly and at times painfully through the woods without his clothes on as it is the result of his sense of communion and identity with the deer. Perhaps the point of the poet's naming specific trees and bushes (oak, fir, laurel, slash pine, thorn) is that the naked man has no opportunity to shrug off or to ignore the woods as though it were merely an undifferentiated mass: it becomes important for him to know which trees and bushes are likely to hurt him as he runs down the mountain.

Wendell Berry has called this poem silly,[2] and, despite Dickey's exposition in *Self-Interviews,* the farfetched plot and the grossly sentimental speaker fail. The persona seems foolish for wanting so much to be a deer that he denies his human dignity. Even he is aware that his effort to be in absolute communion with the deer is wild and futile, for, after his race "Down the shuddering hillside," he speaks of "My brain dazed and pointed with trying / To grow horns, glad that it cannot." The truth is that, however much the poem strives for surrealistic vitality, the deer's image remains a simplistic referent rather than a natural, believable thing: ". . . a deer is created / Descending, then standing and looking. / The sun stands and waits for his horns / / To move." A chaotic poem about chaos is doomed to failure, and Dickey's portrayal of the hunter's straining, creaking, and paunching-up in middle-age is so strained, creaky, and flabby in its language (a coat is "buttoned strainingly," and the hunter's "thighbones groaningly break / Upward") that the poet restores our momentarily suspended disbelief in his fictive world. The speaker of "Springer Mountain" believes at the end that the communion he desired so frenetically for a time is a "dance / Of what I most am and should be," but there is great risk when a person decides that something other than full humanity is better than that humanity, even if a momentary, questionable transcendence is possible through poetry.

Transcendence Unexpected, Enlightenment Unsought. "Chenille" and "Kudzu" both have narrators who are overwhelmed by transcendental vision without having prepared or conditioned themselves in advance. "Chenille" is in part about the transcendence possible to human beings because of their capacity for art. As Dickey says in *Self-Interviews*, "I contrasted the industrial chenille spreads with the spreads produced by the half-demented imagination of this old lady . . . wonderfully symbolic of the artistic process of art produced by the creative mind versus the officialized kind of beauty" (*SI*, 125). But the experience recounted in the poem also makes the point that such transcendence may impinge upon us without our having any expectation whatsoever, as though it were to come in a dream: the animals of the spreads coming to some new life because of their being envisioned by the person who is overlaid by the spreads:

> Someone up there kept throwing
>   Bedspreads upon me.
> Softly I called, and they came:
> The ox and the basilisk,
> The griffin, the phoenix, the lion—
> Light-bodied, only the essence,
> The tufted, creative starfields
> Behind the assembling clouds. . . .

"Chenille" is similar to "In the Marble Quarry" in that the narrator is slightly conscious of his involvement before the actual transcendent vision overtakes him: riding on a stone hoisted from the quarry, the narrator blandly observes "the original shape / Michelangelo believed was in every rock upon earth / . . . heavily stirring, / / Surprised to be an angel." Then he connects himself in an almost off-handed manner with the freed angel: "But no more surprised than I / To feel sadness fall off as though I myself / Were rising from stone. . . ."

"Kudzu" is quite a different story. Setting up a natural creature—a plant—as a kind of encroaching enemy and then bringing on an equivocal savior—pigs—to kill off the serpents hidden in the proliferating kudzu vines, this poem calls up the active transcendence—power and insight—that Dickey is most noted for. From the beginning—"Japan invades"—the poem suggests kudzu's destructiveness. The references to "Far Eastern vines," "Silence that has grown Oriental," and

> . . . the mistaken, mortal
> Arrogance of the snakes
> As the vines, growing insanely, sent
> Great powers into their bodies
> And the freedom to strike without warning. . .

all suggest an unsettling Aryanism which is perhaps understandable if Dickey is being satirical, but which is hardly edifying, even in a World War II pilot who may harbor resentments that noncombatants might not feel. Dickey has said of "The Firebombing" that, referring to John Hersey's novel, it reveals a little of the "War Lover" in him: so does "Kudzu."

But also from the beginning of the poem arises an almost indefinable sense of energy that for Dickey usually implies good. Because of this, the poem maintains an exciting ambivalence toward the defeated enemy—Japan and kudzu-hidden snakes. The end of the poem makes explicit the persona's confrontation with, and participation in, the strength of a vegetable profusion that seems to spawn other life: "From them, though they killed / Your cattle, such energy also flowed / / To you from the knee-high meadow. . . ."

"Kudzu" shows Dickey's habitual use of animals to enliven the plant life in a poem. It is true that the kudzu is, for Dickey and anyone who has had to deal directly with the plant, uncommonly animated vegetation (in some parts of the South its shoots are called "foot-a-nights," to designate their rate of growth in summertime). But it is also true that much of its animation in the poem comes from its physical similarity as well as its ecological proximity to the many snakes which live in its profuse foliage. The scene is additionally vitalized by the savior-pigs who ferociously root out the poisonous serpents. The "purposive" hogs are mock-heroic, comically near-human, an army of "meaty troops" manipulated by the farmer-generals. Personification is rampant, and ironic; even the cows dying of venom are allowed the human capacity of envisioning: ". . . seeing the wood of their stalls / Strain to break into leaf." The poem shows an allegorical flair in its brutal, controlling men; its passive, dying cattle; its devious, deadly snakes; and its single-minded, irresistible pigs. Even though their functions are vivid and specific, they seem in one way unreal, for the narrator busily roots out *Meaning,* makes his explicit correspondences finally seem more important than the mundane images: "You live inside your frail house, / And you think, in the opened cold, / Of the surfaces of things and its terrors." But the trigger to the poem, its original image, is in the volition of the vines themselves, not in the purposeful seeking of the human narrator: they "invade"; "you must close your windows / / At night to keep it out of the house"; and so forth. The original vitality of the image is within the plant itself, not just in the meaning-hungry mind of the narrator.

Mystical Possession: The Volition of The Other.   "Approaching Prayer" opens with the clear indication that true inspiration comes from somewhere outside the control of the person involved:

> A moment tries to come in
> Through the windows, when one must go
> Beyond what there is in the room,
>
> But it must come straight down.

The force of epiphany comes from outside and *up* somewhere: this poem is directly religious, as the title indicates, but it resists the collapsing of this natural world into vague spirituality. The speaker knows firmly that he must act now that the "moment" has come.

Sensing that his new knowledge and its expression are beyond reason and conventional language, the narrator turns to overt ritual. He makes his way to the attic, where he finds several articles—his father's sweater, "The spurs of his gamecock," and "the head of a boar / I once helped to kill with two arrows"—which lead the son to imagine his father's and the boar's experiences, such blood-thrill as hunting and cock-fighting may impart. Eventually he does

> . . . put on the ravelled nerves [the sweater]
>
> And gray hairs of my tall father
> In the dry grave growing like fleece,
> Strap his bird spurs to my heels
> And kneel down under the skylight.

At last, he dons the "hollow hog's head / Gazing straight up / With star points in the glass eyes. . . ." The effect of his disguise, his ritual dress, is, as in "Armor," for the person to take on attributes of the helmet: the son imagines he is the hunted boar.

Moving through roman and italic typographic variations similar to those in Faulkner's prose and Melville's poetry, Dickey strives for mystical simultaneity: the son is both animal and man, father and child, the hunter and the hunted. He is suspended, as in Eliot's "still point": "Beasts, angels, / I am nearly that motionless now"; "The moon and the stars do not move."

Richard Howard has written of Dickey's use of helmets, "One of the principal *images of earth* Dickey has always used is that of the helmet. . . : the word itself derives from two old verbs for protecting and concealing— protection, in Dickey's world, against the energies of the earth, and concealment against those of the Unseen, crown and prison both."[3] But such etymology is misleading, for Dickey perceives helmet (or armor) as a place of seeing-again, a center for reenvisioning the familiar. It is part of his scheme of seeking transcendence that a person must turn the familiar world around in new light, shift it out of its well-known foci, and view it from standpoints never before attempted. Helmets are for protection and concealment, but to Dickey they are also a means to greater vulnerability. To helmet oneself in the apprehension of touching the heart-spirit is not to hide; it is an act of risk, of daring, for the poet who wants not just to make poems but to live an energized life, which includes poetry.

"Approaching Prayer" concludes cautiously, with the speaker knowing what he knows, but not making undue claims of prophetic authority. He even specifies, in the calm later recollection, certain qualities that allowed his mystical ritual to succeed insofar as it did:

> . . . I can say only, and truly,
> That my stillness was violent enough,
> That my brain had blood enough,
> That my right hand was steady enough,
> That the warmth of my father's wool grave

> Imparted love enough
> And the keen heels of feathery slaughter
> Provided lift enough,
> That reason was dead enough
> For something important to be:
>
> That, if not heard,
> It may have been somehow said.

In fact, in most of Dickey's poems that deal with a person's effort to have and to sustain a transcendental experience, the final tone is of at least partial disappointment—"love's sad satiety," as Shelley wrote in "To a Skylark." "Bums, on Waking" ("They expect and hope for / / Something totally other"), "Goodbye to Serpents" ("And I know I have not been moved / Enough by the things I have moved through"), and even the Christly, heroic figure of "A Folk Singer of the Thirties" ("This is all a thing I began / To believe, to change, and to sell / When I opened my mouth to the rich")—all three poems work through their transcendence and come out with their speakers altered but still human, still subject to the dangers of everyday pressures, of the mundane cloud around social groups, of the sheer laziness of mind and body. Dickey is not one to see the world cheaply, with glazed-over romantic eyes and singing misty songs to blot the noises of the harsh world: he shows in his poems that transcendent experiences, however mystically and mysteriously thay may come, must be actively held and sustained if humankind is to be most fully human. There is otherwise too much threat of extinction, too much certainty of oblivion. And Dickey proclaims survivorship that is based on human beings' coming to a physical and spiritual synthesis that all too often is ignored in the pursuits of material—or weak, ephemeral spiritual—goals.

One of Dickey's best poems about transcendence as mystical possession is "Drinking from a Helmet," and part of its success may be ascribed to the continual concrete associations that the poet maintains with what he knows to have been at one time a real soldier, a man who is now dead. This is not a vague, self-indulgent poem like "The Being"; rather, this first-person narrator mystically identifies with a dead person whose helmet he now wears, and he thereby is turned profoundly into himself and outward into a spirit of comradeship with all mortals. The poem brings together Dickey's sense of survival in war (*SI*, 135–36) and his guilt and wonder at being born at all. It links birth and growing up with the spirits of the dead, who are our foundation of humanity. In earlier poems, Dickey's brother is metaphorically integral with vegetation images; in "Drinking from a Helmet" there is the exciting juxtaposition of giant redwoods and the imagined meeting of two brothers, one of whom has found a proxy-after-death in the persona of the poem. This work does not refer explicitly to his brother, but Dickey manages to harness the force of his own family history to compel his reader to a sense of general brotherhood and general mortality.

"The Being" portrays a man's possession by a fearsome, ghostly Otherness that seems to have no direct relation to any specific, identifiable dead person. The implication is that people sometimes are overpowered by feelings or presences that they cannot identify as *themselves*. One might say that such possessions are entirely subjective—fantasies—but one function of poetry is for a poet to express what he feels; and in this poem Dickey tells of feeling that he is possessed from outside himself and that he has no control over the possessing spirit.

There is a truly omnipresent Other in the poem ("It is there, above him, beyond, behind, / Distant, and near"), but, as in "Approaching Prayer," there is also a linear motion toward the speaker: "Something fills the bed he has been / Able only to half-fill." The sleeper stirs and appears completely, inexplicably restless until the fourth stanza, when he "breaks into sweat from his heart / All over his body / In something's hands." This unsought impingement of the Other upon an unexpectant person is prelude to epiphany: "he is now, seeing straight / Through the roof wide   wider / / Wide awake."

"The Being" seems clearly sexual in its invasion; and the dreadful nature of the Other, coupled with the seemingly joyous laughter evoked by it, suggests that a systematic Freudian reading of Dickey would prove enlightening. The poet himself has commented:

"The Being" is a poem unlike most of mine. Figure a man who is sleeping on a winter night and is being possessed by something. He doesn't know whether it's a human woman who gets into bed with him or a succubus—a mythological creature who co-habits with sleeping men and takes their energy—or whether it's an angel or some kind of renewing spirit of the year. I deliberately did not explain what it was, because when you have these visitations, as sometimes happens, the whole point is that you don't know whether it's a dream or what. It's all of these things and none of them. But the experience in the poem is definitely meant to be sexual and has not so much the effect of robbing the sleeper of his powers as being a kind of purgation of the winter's ills and a presage of the spring's renewal. (*SI*, 133–34)

Dickey's observation that M. L. Rosenthal is "the only critic who mentions 'The Being'" (*SI,* 134) suggests that he wanted the poem to do more, alas, than it does. Filled with clichés ("He turns and buries his head"; "He goes rigid / And breaks into sweat"), it strains after mystery, and stands notably impoverished in its diction. Perhaps the use of third-person narrative is a flaw: so much of the immediacy of the experience depends upon the reader's strong empathy with the sleeper-dreamer-mystic Dickey tries to portray. Mostly, though, the problem is one that does not usually affect James Dickey: the imagery is simply not enough to sustain the subjective feelings of this work. The fear of not surviving, of perhaps losing "powers," is too arbitrarily asserted: the drama is too flimsily embodied.

"The Being" remains "interesting," like "The Vegetable King" and "The Other," whose "green of excess" ("Springer Mountain") promises energy-to-be-refined. And "Drinking from a Helmet" does fulfill much of its promise of mystico-sexual imagery. Later, with "May Day Sermon" and "Falling" breaking all sorts of boundaries of thought and form, "The Being" is somewhat justified—ransomed—for its foreshadowing. Certainly it is a poem whose impulse and execution expand away from the masterly precisions of other poems about fear and survivorship, such as "The Driver," "Horses and Prisoners," and "The Scarred Girl." It explores new ranges of artistic accomplishment that the cautious forms and subjects of *Into the Stone* could hardly have surveyed. But its aspiration to transcendence is frustrated, not up to the quality of the best poems of *Helmets*.

Buckdancer's Choice (1965)

Family, with a More Objective Eye.   Except for "The Ice Skin," "In the Child's Night," and "Approaching Prayer," *Helmets* departed from the theme of family that had so much occupied Dickey's attention in his first two books. *Buckdancer's Choice*—winner of the National Book Award in 1966—returned to focus on it with great precision and poignant restraint: two poems about his mother ("Angina" and "Buckdancer's Choice"), one about his father and mother together ("The Celebration"), and two others—"The Second Sleep" and "The Aura"—conjoined for this book under the title "Fathers and Sons."

Of these five poems, four are most concerned with the death of a family member: only "The Celebration"—appropriately—concentrates on the living. Its simple scene presents the grown son, the poet, meandering through a carnival when he discovers that his mother and father are there, enjoying themselves: "I believed them buried miles back / In the country, in the faint sleep / Of the old. . . ." The parents ascend the ferris wheel, to the astonishment of the son, who suddenly perceives their happiness ("Understanding the whirling impulse / From which I had been born") outside their relationship with him ("All this having all and nothing / To do with me"). With this new, mature joy the result of learning his separateness, he "became / In five strides a kind of loving, / A mortal, a dutiful son."

"Angina," however, with its much looser lines and its struggling with painful subject matter—the impending death of one's own mother—makes its tender message with cautiously sententious declarative sentences: "Death in the heart must be calm, / / Must not look suddenly"; "Existence is family." "Angina" is a gentle poem, with the speaker being careful not to break into unfit emotional display, but also not wanting to be cold: "I must be still and not worry, / Not worry, not worry, to hold / My peace, my poor place, my own." With these quiet, tense repetitions, Dickey reaches a particular genuine sentiment that he touches nowhere else in his work.

"Buckdancer's Choice" is also about the dying mother, but its angle of vision is quite different from that of "Angina." More like "The Performance," with its sense of mission to the survivors of the world, "Buckdancer's Choice" draws a conclusion that is firm from its beginning: "So I would hear out those lungs," the speaker says in his first line, to give readers notice that this poem of three-line stanzas is tough-minded and ready to tell someone's hard-earned message. The mother "Was dying of breathless angina, / / Yet still found breath enough / To whistle. . . ." The speaker is summoned by her tune to envision "the classic buck-and-wing men / / Of traveling minstrel shows," but the poem chiefly synthesizes the woman with those old-time entertainers. She whistles even when no one is in the room with her; the son "crept close to the wall" to listen as the brave music of the woman's breath went forth—like Donald Armstrong's final handstands and kip-up in "The Performance"—to do "All things in this life that [she] could." Her music comes in the poem to symbolize her vigorous, almost evangelical spirit:

> Proclaiming what choices there are
> For the last dancers of their kind,
>
> For ill women and for all slaves
> Of death, and children enchanted at walls. . . .

In "The Second Sleep" Dickey blends the dream of a son with the sound of the automobile accident "three blocks to the north" which kills his father. The son's dream is of himself as a deer in mating season hearing "An animal clash, a shock of resolving antlers" and finding himself amid a "herd of does," which turn out to be "The next room filled with women."

When he is awakened, the scene pulls too abruptly back to reality for the reader to have much emotional investment in the death of the father, described in the poem only as "A gentle man," who "liftingly strained / And carried [the son] to the next room," sometime before the accident. The poem very formally alternates its one- and two-line stanzas, but the formal restraint does not convey or create emotional pressure. The father simply does not matter very much.

"The Aura" turns the subject around somewhat, with the boy apparently "broken on the road" as he rode in "his last year / Of bicycles." The father is haunted by his memory of the son's "aura" of music: "his portable radio always / At his belt, leaning over, adjusting the dial. . . ." The sensitivity the father has after the son's death is demonstrated in his precise perception of music at home and in public places: "That sound is the same, and yet not— / There is too much steadiness in it: none / Is carried rightly. . . ." The son is not remembered in some static image or sensation, but rather in his recollected motion: "And now the sound still coming / From everywhere is grief. / Unstoppable." The poem closes, like "Fog Envelops the Animals," with so strong an apprehension of *qualities* that the syntax compresses into fragments: "Bongoes. Steel / Guitars. A precious cheapness / He would have grown out of. Something. Music."

The Hunt, under Threat.   Dickey's belief that *Helmets* is about hunting is partially fulfilled by the time of *Buckdancer's Choice,* when Dickey's nature imagery is entirely dominated by animate creatures. But the hunting is turned to the animals' side. While *Helmets* included the startling vivacity of "Kudzu," to draw his vegetation to its poetic climax, and "Springer Mountain," whose narrator and sentiments both "limp" to their bland conclusions, *Buckdancer's Choice* produced three memorable poems about animate life at its most sinister—a killer whale, a rattlesnake, and a hammerhead shark—to designate the world of Dickey's darker imagination. Transcendence is not always a thing of joy. Sometimes to "cross over" is to probe the darkness, or to have the abyss stare back. As the vegetation disappears, so does the cautious poet. In *Buckdancer's Choice* he grows more dramatic in subject matter and more decisive, active, less reflexive in attitude, as though time were closing down to make life and poetry matter more than ever.

At its simplest level, "Pursuit from Under" is narrated by a man who, as a youngster, became possessed in fantasy by the tragic story found in the diary of "Arctic explorers" who starved to death on an expedition. But the poem refuses to lie only at that simplest level; the fearsome shadow of an aggressive killer whale beneath the ice becomes a symbol—a moving, living thing that is the Destroyer, the Death-bringer (even though the explorers actually starve to death: they are not attacked by the whale): "If you run, he will follow you. . . ." This Melvillean whale is a symbol to the narrator, as it was to the expeditioners before him: "They had been given an image / Of how the downed dead pursue us." In this poem, death is not a fixed and static condition; it is a moving, hunting creature: "not only in the snow / But in the family field / / The small shadow moves. . . ." Motion, for Dickey, is the manifestation of life-process, which includes an almost spiritualistic continuity of the dead in the world of the living: ". . . somewhere the turf will heave, / And the outraged breath of the dead, / So long held, will form / / Unbreathably around the living. . . ." Death, in order to find and destroy the active Dickey-persona, must itself be active, not just a condition of slowing and ossifying, resulting in final stasis. As "Fog Envelops the Animals" showed earlier, Dickey's terrors (and certain joys, as in *Deliverance*) are in whatever actively hunts him down.

"Pursuit from Under" is unusual in Dickey's work, for its specification of death through the experience of someone else, the now-dead, whose very words up to the time of their deaths the narrator still possesses. (This depiction of premortem thoughts is brought to culmination in "Falling.") It is not a study of "how we should live or die" (as in "The Performance" or "Buckdancer's Choice") so much as of the fact of death itself. Despite its somewhat morbid concentration on the death experience, the frightening whale, and the strengthless dead, this poem works a marvelous charm in its fusion of the spirits of the dead—somehow still alive in the world—and the terror of being hunted by an inevitable killer.

It is this sinister aspect of the physical world, this transformation of the theme of hunting into general threat, that comes to maturity in Dickey's work after *Helmets*. "Reincarnation"—called "(I)" after the publication of "Reincarnation (II)"—pictures a rattlesnake as the embodiment of some former human being: "This one is feeling his life as a man move slowly away. / Fallen from that estate, he has gone down on his knees. . . ." The primary image (easily come by) recalls the serpent of Eden, cursed ever after his treachery to crawl on his belly in the dust. Dickey shows the snake as a hunter with purely murderous intentions: "waiting—all the time a symbol of evil— / Not for food, but for the first man to walk by the gentle river. . . ." Although the accuracy of the rattlesnake's being born oviparously (unlike many snakes, they are born "live") has been refuted in Harry Morris's "thoroughly jaundiced view of Dickey's work,"[4] the snake's wanting "to pass on, handless, what yet may be transferred / In a sudden giving-withdrawing move, like a country judge striking a match," engenders a strong imagistic response. Less a matter of real transcendence— thus unlike "Reincarnation (II)"—this poem serves to clarify a philosophical-theological point. An emblem poem of sorts, it forces a rational mold over the inchoate, anxious sense of ultimate judgment and the prospects of mortal fragility.

"The Shark's Parlor," one of Dickey's best comic poems, captures, with the narrative verve of "Cherrylog Road," a risky experience that clearly gets out of hand and becomes destructive. Basically, the plot is simple. A young man and his friend, Payton Ford, set an oversized hookline and attach it to "a spindling porch pillar" of their beach house. A shark takes the hook, bends the house, and causes general panic before it is towed through the house by the young men and "all other haulers" summoned from the town: "The screen door banged and tore off   he scrambled on his tail   slid / Curved   did a thing from another world. . . ."

As vivid as this story is, however, its main point has to do with the way the person's mind responds, through memory, with the same sort of physical excitement that the original experience evokes. "The Shark's Parlor" indicates that the men ironically take the beast out of its parlor into theirs, but they have "dreamed of the great fin circling / Under the bedroom floor" before they ever imagine they would have the shark in their "vacation paradise   cutting all four legs from under the dinner table." The effect of the ocean so close is to heighten the poet's sense of otherness. That awareness thoroughly dominates the early Dickey poems in terms of some named and some unnamed ghostly presences, but here the immanent spirit of nature is given a form—however phantasmic—to symbolize the powers in the vast natural sea. The poem emphasizes the "blue blazing terror" of the difference between the "water it was in" and "the human house," which seems so safe until the hammerhead is towed through it. After the shark is beached and killed, its body is released again to the water. But the narrator is not through: "What could I do but buy / That house. . . ?" "Blood hard as iron on the wall" keeps the recollection keen, and memory gives the person new rights to wholeness: "all changes: Memory: / Something like three-dimensional dancing in the limbs   with age / Feeling more in two worlds than one   in all worlds the growing encounter." However tough the fight waged against all the rope-pulling force of these people, the shark dies. Nonetheless, the total energy of nature's spirit is undiminished. At the same time as the narrator recognizes this fact, he not only apprehends the force of the nature Out There; he also sees that his own human nature is part of the otherness, that the unity of the vital, animate forces of the universe is truly overwhelming, awesome as the fear of God.

Sexuality: Joy, Threat, the Twistings of Desire. Philosophically, Dickey aspires to unrestrained access to all things natural, including (perhaps especially) sexuality. As it turns out, many of his sexual poems are about hunting, as well—the pursuit; illicit, sometimes even perverse, relationships that have more promise of the glorious moment than of long-lasting commitment. One unfailing success at public readings is the comic "Cherrylog Road," which appears in *Helmets,* but which serves here as a bridge to other, more complex works in *Buckdancer's Choice.* Despite Benjamin DeMott's comment that it does not "clarify experience substantially,"[5] it is a minor masterpiece of poetic narrative, whose skillfully unobtrusive technique replicates the premeditated but passionate sexual encounter of two young people in a junkyard.

Beginning in relatively slow motion, its images alternate between stasis (or slowness) and sometimes rapid motion. The total effect is exhilarating: "Off Highway 106 / At Cherrylog Road I entered / The '34 Ford without wheels," the narrator says, "With a seat pulled out to run / Corn whiskey down from the hills." The junked cars are "Smothered in kudzu" and "Reared up on . . . building blocks," but in the midst of this clutter and decay the boy is mostly confident that "Doris Holbrook / Would escape from her father at noon." Exercising what he calls elsewhere "Gigantic forepleasure" ("Adultery," *P,* 259), Dickey delays her entrance until two-thirds through the poem. Doris eludes her possessive father, pretending to him to scavenge in the wreckage: "To seek parts owned by the sun / Among the abandoned chassis." In one long sentence—twenty-two pell-mell lines—Dickey gives a funny description of the destruction that not decay but Doris, wrench in hand, wreaks upon the junked cars, and ends with her blood-vengeful father in a seriocomic image that only years of the young man's retrospect could have retrieved from full-blown nightmare.

With their sexual consummation, its powerful tension and union obliterating whatever connotations of stasis that the word "held" might have held, the narrator propels readers and junkyard alike into passionate action:

> I held her and held her and held her,
> Convoyed at terrific speed
> By the stalled, dreaming traffic around us,
> So the blacksnake, stiff
> With inaction, curved back
> Into life and hunted the mouse
>
> With deadly excitement,
> The beetles reclaimed their field. . . .

The vermin, the rusted seat-springs, the motionless car doors, all are transformed by the young lovers into something moving and vital: "We left by separate doors / Into the changed, other bodies / Of cars."

DeMott's charge that the poem "ends thinly"[6] is partly a consequence of the tactic that Dickey adopted to give the poem its feeling of headlong motion, thus preempting any dedicated farewell of the two lovers. The junkyard's soul is "restored," and the motorcycling young man is "Wild to be wreckage forever," exuberant testimony to the incongruous site of love-in-wreckage that has germinated the poem. "Cherrylog Road" draws much of its energy from the fact that the young persons' liaison is illicit, and the unwholesome wrath of Mr. Holbrook is a large factor in generating reader sympathy for them: his angry, threatening presence also helps titillate the boy and girl in their adventure. But, most importantly, this quite premeditated tryst has an appealing air of passion that is a direct result of Dickey's syntax and his images of motion and stasis, which press his narrative precipitously forward.

The momentum of "Cherrylog Road" is a function of the story's joyous, uncontainable natural bounty, but sometimes uncontained passions grow dangerous. Although many of Dickey's earlier poems portray darker elements of the natural world—"Walking on Water," "The Owl King," and "Kudzu," for example—few of his love poems suggest real danger. "Awaiting the Swimmer" (*Into the Stone*) says of the swimming woman, "Her best motions come from the river; / / Her fear flows away to the sea"; and "Cherrylog Road" strikes this terrifying portrait of the girl's father. But with the former poem, fear seems to be posed by the natural world—the threatening mortal symbol of the flowing river—and with the latter, danger is objectified in the father. In "The Fiend" (*Buckdancer's Choice*), Dickey first shows the passion itself to be fearsome.

"The Fiend" himself, "a worried accountant," wears a "seersucker suit" and is bluntly called "a solid citizen." So, although he is something of a stereotypical "creep," he is visibly innocuous, not a wild-eyed maniac universally suspected of violence. He climbs a tree to peer into the window of a woman who is undressing. While there, he seems to draw energy from the tree, but more conspicuously the natural objects (fallaciously) sympathize:

> . . . When she gives up
> Her aqua terry-cloth robe the wind quits in mid-tree   the birds
> Freeze to their perches   round his head   a purely human light
> Comes out of a one-man oak   around her an energy field   she stands
> Rooted. . . .

This is a man from whose mind nothing could be more distant than murder, but the poet keeps touching, barely touching, the motif: "the knife / And flicks it open   it glints on the moon one time"; "It will be something small that sets him off: / Perhaps a pair of lace pants on a clothesline"; and "he will casually follow her in   like a door-to-door salesman / The godlike movement of trees stiffening with him   the light / Of a hundred favored windows   gone wrong somewhere in his glasses. . . ." Again and again, Dickey's third-person voice speaks, almost comradely, as though the poem were in first person, telling the favorable effects of voyeurism. The man is "renewed," makes "a final declaration / Of love," and actually believes that "It is his beholding that saves them: / God help the dweller in windowless basements." He is identified in part with good, natural instincts: "the dog's honest eyes and the man's the same pure beast's / Comprehending the same essentials."

The fiend knows that "Not one of these beheld would ever give / Him a second look   but he gives them all a first look that goes / On and on   conferring immortality while it lasts. . . ." His idealization of women results in a curious protectiveness, a skewed paternalism that shows up in some of Dickey's other works, early and late—"Cherrylog Road," "May Day Sermon," and "Blood." This poet is remarkable in his ability to teeter on the brink of perversity and yet hold balance enough to maintain readers' interest and empathy. "The Fiend" is one of his most notable poems, both technically and in terms of content: like "Falling," it might be called the kind of poem that only James Dickey could get away with.

Guilt Again: The Social Response.   While the point of view of "The Fiend" conveys no sense of personal guilt, the first and last poems of *Buckdancer's Choice* do so quite directly: "The Firebombing," with guilt over war and the warrior's paradoxical inability to feel guilt; and "Slave Quarters," with guilt over racial exploitation and the consequences of certain kinds of sexual transgression. Richard Howard writes that "The Firebombing" "is, surely, Dickey's most complete statement of the magical life in its appalling triumphs (military rank and power a part of the Old Order of kingship and vassalage) over against the slow conquests and defeats of an undistinguished reality. . . . The burden [of 'Slave Quarters'] is the same . . . ; 'How to take on guilt'; and the shock of recognition which the present must sustain when confronted by the old dispensation, the magical immoralities of the past, is the same too."[7]

"The Firebombing" is perhaps the strongest single refutation of charges by critics like Robert Bly, who called Dickey at least thoughtless and irresponsible and at worst evil for being uninvolved in the active social and political movements of the 1960s and 1970s.[8] The epigraph, from Günter Eich, clearly indicates that the poet is aware of the disclaimers of guilt offered by all participants in war ("Think on it, that for the huge destroying / Every man bemoans that he was innocent"); but, Dickey says in *Self-Interviews*, "In poems, and elsewhere, it's very easy to abase yourself and be terribly guilty over your own or somebody else's warlike actions" (*SI*, 137). Dickey's intense feelings about the subject are made clear in the scorn which he levels upon easy guilt-people: "It's fashionable to talk about guilt in poems, like Sylvia Plath feeling guilty over the slaughter of the Jews. She didn't have anything to do with it. She can be *sorry*, but guilt is more personal than that: it has to do with something you have *done*, or could have done and didn't. It's a literary convention for her. To have guilt you've got to earn guilt, but sometimes when you earn it, you don't feel the guilt you ought to have. And that's what 'The Firebombing' is about" (*SI*, 137).

The poem itself affects a kind of dissociation of the poet from the character he describes, who seems plainly to be himself, twenty years before. Richard Howard bluntly calls the narrator "he the poet James Dickey, no other man,"[9] while the narrator speaks of "some technical-minded stranger with my hands." The man in the poem, be he Dickey himself or not, comes to the reader as a character in a personal drama: a trauma of memory and re-evaluation. "Homeowners unite," he says in line one, stressing his identity with the general suburban population. But the distances of time and space from his particular past make him face questions that—whether others have similar problems or not—he must resolve absolutely for himself. He generalizes, "All families lie together, though some are burned alive. / The others try to feel / For them. Some can, it is often said." And when he is done with this brief exercise of objectifying, he speaks imperatively to himself to begin his very purposeful daydream: "Starve and take off / / Twenty years in the suburbs. . . ."

He recalls—and relives—his sense of power and ecstasy as he flew missions in his night-fighter-bombers over Japan. He moves occasionally in and out of his suburban setting, trying desperately to envision the effects of bombing as if they had occurred to his own habitation. He speaks humorously but derogatorily of his life, "Where the lawn mower rests on its laurels / Where the diet exists / For my own good. . . ." He turns a critical eye—with his own quotation marks—to himself "In the air above Beppu / For I am fulfilling / / An 'anti-morale' raid upon it." Later, imagining in much detail the "red costly blast / Flinging jelly over the walls," he quails, "My hat should crawl on my head / In streetcars, thinking of it, / The fat on my body should pale."

But with all the lurid imagery of war's effects upon civilians, the poet remains, it seems, most concerned at his inability to sympathize enough, to know as much as he feels he should about his victims, to feel guilty enough:

> It is this detachment,
> The honored aesthetic evil,
> The greatest sense of power in one's life,
> That must be shed in bars, or by whatever
> Means. . . .

The lust for cool and honorific power which has devolved upon the modern warrior runs sadly counter to the sentiments expressed in a poem by one of Dickey's earliest literary interests, Herman Melville. In "A Utilitarian View of the Monitor's Fight," Melville's expectation is that war made grimy and technological would lose its glory and thus pass out of favor and practice with men. The horror of Dickey's poem lies in the fact that Melville is proved utterly wrong: the new glory is in the ecstasy of powerful, inhuman detachment. Dickey's narrator is a caught creature; human decency conflicts absolutely with patriotic duty. After all the effort of Dickey's eight-page poem, after all the terrible imagery of war's destruction, all the correspondences drawn between the suburban ease of the American narrator, the despair is in his recognition that no mere memory or sheer imagining can fully, truly compensate for deeds done in that past. Dickey's narrator closes in one of the most honest but chilling confessions in modern poetry:

> . . . It is that I can imagine
> At the threshold nothing
> With its ears crackling off
> Like powdery leaves,
> Nothing with children of ashes, nothing not
> Amiable, gentle, well-meaning,
> A little nervous for no
> Reason   a little worried   a little too loud
> Or too easygoing   nothing I haven't lived with
> For twenty years, still nothing not as
> American as I am, and proud of it.
>
> Absolution? Sentence? No matter;
> The thing itself is in that.

In "Slave Quarters," the last poem in *Buckdancer's Choice,* Dickey also tries to relive events of the past, in this case, the guilty deeds and remorse of his southern plantation-owner ancestors. But he makes it clear to the reader that this reliving is a willful act of the imagination—overwhelming in its emotional impact upon the speaker of the poem, yes, but nonetheless imagined and willed. He says, "I feel my imagining loins / Rise"; he tells things he can do ("I can pull"; "I can begin to dance"); and he orders things to happen ("Ah, stand up / Blond loins"; "Let Africa rise upon me like a man"). But the main proof of his aesthetic detachment is in the last stanza, when the speaker admits his volition in "thinking about" the guilty past of southern white men (an especially troubling subject in light of Dickey's remarks about Sylvia Plath's imagined guilt over the Jews). Thus, this poem portrays not spiritualistic possession—as we have seen elsewhere in *Helmets* and *Buckdancer's Choice*—but rather a sensitive man's imagining, and empathizing with, the terrible plight of a white father-owner and a brown son-slave in the Old South. The poem brings together Dickey's various senses of guilt—the social order's demands and expectations of immoral acts, the sexual exercise of dominant men, the personal wrong done to one's own blood-kin (here a son, rather than a brother)—the spirits of the dead who are still with us, the effortful transcendence that sometimes one might aspire to, and the limitations of imagination. One cannot actually live the deeds—guilty or not—of past time. (Maybe this poem more than any other of Dickey's suggests the preciosity of poetic straining, more than "Springer Mountain," because the whole effort here is in the mind, not in the physical acts of that lumbering lubbard of a middle-aged hunter.)

Finally, though, this poem serves as a compendium of the major themes of Dickey's middle period. The poet stands on a plot of ground amid the imagined environs of the old plantation house; struck by the image of himself there, he draws together the present and two hundred years past. Stunned at the end by the vision of his own brown son, the present-day narrator resorts to rhetorical questions to conclude the epiphany. Willfully pressing himself to transcendence, instructing aloud his own body to perform the deeds of his racial past, insisting upon his continuity with the ancestral men who rebuffed the wilderness of sawgrass, and clearly blending the moon of his real and imagined skies, the speaker turns the world into a thing it has never been before. The daring to enter the spirit-world of historical past puts the speaker at least momentarily at the mercy of the characters of his mind, allowing the nervously thin white wife to read his deceptions in the shadows he traverses to the slave yard, where another woman makes his blonde loins rise toward her darkness, whence emerges the son of his possession whom he cannot name as his. The family he gets is not like Dickey's much-acknowledged one in other poems in these two volumes; but the impulse to blood-union is impressive, and the need to gather family close transcends even two centuries' expanse. The sexual motive is blatant in this poem, and the twisted use of slaves as sexual partners recalls the needs not of the headlong, joyous boy and girl in "Cherrylog Road" but rather the destructive desperation of "The Fiend." The really new element, though, is that of guilt in response to sexual activity, or, more accurately, guilt in recognition of the consequences of progeny—when in a society where one may not, one has a son. The guilt is personal in the poem; the two-hundred-year-old secret is presumably safe-kept. The poem both preserves and insulates.

Chapter Five

The Long Sermon and the Long Fall: Transcendence by Means of Excess

In his highly critical essay "James Dickey: Meter and Structure," Paul Ramsey declares, "The metrical history of James Dickey can be put briefly and sadly: a great lyric rhythm found him; he varied it, loosened it, then left it, to try an inferior form."[1] Laurence Lieberman, on the other hand, in "Notes on James Dickey's Style," speaks admiringly of poems in *Buckdancer's Choice* and *Falling*: "This form adapts perfectly to a welter of experience in flux. The rhetoric keeps drawing more and more live matter into the poem, as from a boundless supply. . . . The Verse paragraph break is never a true interruption to the rhythmic sweep of the phrase-chain. It merely suggests a shift in perspective, a slowing down and speeding up of the unstoppable momentum, an occasional amplification of the breath-spaces that already separate every phrase from phrase."[2] The point finally does come, perhaps, to a matter of taste; but attention to a poet's style that does not acknowledge the poetic mission attempted in each work is likely to be a faulty enterprise. James Dickey's later poems become looser, more effusive, more expansive, more prosaic, more oratorical because his felt mission becomes less that of tautly strung introspection and more that of the energetic visionary, the expansive, Faustian embracer of all things, including—and maybe especially—the wild and dangerous. At times ridiculous, bombastic, and prolix, Dickey's long-line works demand the reader's indulgence. Such letting go yields treasures unimagined by safe and managerial minds.

"May Day Sermon to the Women of Gilmer County, Georgia, by a Woman Preacher Leaving the Baptist Church"

Ill-served by Ramsey's description, "the sexual-hysterical rantings of an insane woman preacher,"[3] "May Day Sermon" generates mythic overtones that are absolutely dependent upon oratorical excesses. The backwoods preacher has lately discovered the cruel influences of the Old Testament Jehovah upon possessive, sadistic fathers whose newly sexual daughters slip away to the embraces of their young lovers. She preaches about the recurrence of the springtime fervor, the youngsters' coming annually to new and renewed sexual urgency; and in the course of her warning of that urgency, she recounts a mythical story of a young girl whose father beats her viciously while she is chained helpless to a tractor in the barn. The girl so violently punished turns violent herself, kills her father, and runs off with her motorcyclist lover, having also released all the farm animals to roam loose into the foggy land. This is no story to be tightly constrained. And it is a story whose *telling* is as important as the actual events within its plot. Jane Bowers Martin notes that

Dickey's drafts of "May Day Sermon" reveal that he thought of the poem as legend from the earliest stages—two of the working titles were "A May Day Courtship Legend" and "A Courtship Legend of Gilmer County." More importantly, the drafts reveal that Dickey was well into the poem (which is 403 pages in draft) before he decided to use the woman preacher as narrator. The introduction of the poetic narrator as legend bearer is essential to successful transcendence through legend within the framework of poetry. Just as the sheep child's status as legend is not accomplished by the sheep child himself but by the farm boy, so it was necessary for Dickey to find a narrator suitable for perpetuating the legend of the "May Day Sermon" lovers.[4]

The woman preacher begins her sermon by directly referring to her own role: "Each year at this time I shall be telling you of the Lord / —Fog, gamecock, snake and neighbor—giving men all the help they need / To drag their daughters into barns." "Children," she says at first, and later, "Sisters." She refers again and again to "telling" ("listen"; "I shall be telling"), and she ultimately identifies with the very girl whose supposedly sinful deeds are being chastised: "telling you not to believe every scream you hear / Is the Bible's: it may be you or me   it may be her sinful barn- / howling for the serpent, as her father whips her." The passion that the preacher is describing—and in fact living herself through her own oratory—is clearly seen to be the life-force much more holy than the rampant religiosity of fathers over their women.

The tension is a thing of the group listening, not just that of a reader alone, or that of a speaker alone: it is like the rhythmic progressions of late-night AM-radio preachers everywhere. This woman preacher's consciousness of herself as one who is caught up in the passion of her story is exactly what forces her to leave the Baptist Church: her sermon has taught her to love the natural passions more than the unnatural ravaging of kin by malicious and misguided zealots. As she reports the entrance of the motorcycle lover, one might read her lines as truly prohibitive, as though the women should learn a lesson and stay away from such as he: "Ah, children, / There is now something else to hear: there is now this madness of engine / Noise in the bushes   past reason   ungodly   squealing." Even later, when the preacher's syntax grows more exclamatory, the lines might still indicate her disapproval, even her fear of this devilish man on the hog of an engine: "O daughters   his heartbeat great / With trees   some blue leaves coming   NOW   and right away fire / In the right eye   Lord   more MORE O Glory   land / Of Glory." But by the time she has begun to speak in specifically sexual terms ("His rubber stiffens on its nails"), her turn of mind is evident: the truest passionate response to the Lord, for her, is to rejoice in the fusion of these lovers' story and the springtime rejuvenescence:

>   . . . Sisters, understand about men and sheaths:
>
> About nakedness: understand how butterflies, amazed, pass out
> Of their natal silks   how the tight snake takes a great breath
>   bursts
> Through himself and leaves himself behind   how a man casts
>   finally
> Off everything that shields him from another   beholds his
>   loins
> Shine with his children forever   burn with the very juice
> Of resurrection. . . .

By such extraordinary means—the violence upon the girl by her father, the murder of the father, the wild rescue and escape on the motorcycle, the releasing of the farm animals, and the imaginative participation and "conversion" of the woman preacher by this story—Dickey allows the lovers, the preacher, and to some extent his readers to transcend everyday expectations of the self, submission to unrighteous cruelty, and conventional prohibitions against the rebellion of women, particularly, against the dominations of doctrine and of physical force. His poem describes and ritualizes the transcendence possible through connection with natural forces and through the exercise of artful oratory and legendry.

"The Sheep Child" as Touchstone of Transcendence

"May Day Sermon" and *Falling* (a group of twenty-three poems) appear in book form first in *Poems 1957–1967,* the former at the very beginning of the volume and the latter at the end. *Falling* opens with "Reincarnation (II)," which is told from the point of view of a seabird who is a reincarnated human being. As the poem progresses, the human qualities fade and the instinctual qualities of the bird grow dominant. Dickey has said that the poem conveys his long-felt desire to fly without the apparatus of aircraft (*SI,* 61), and the poem is somewhat successful in its suggestion of nonrational thought and sensuous apprehensions one might attribute to a bird. But he does strain for the effect. The first poem in Section II is "The Sheep Child," which Dickey has said is the poem on which he will "stand or fall."[5] In it the sort of transcendent vision Dickey aspires to in fusing the human and nonhuman worlds in his two "Reincarnation" poems comes forth almost perfectly: the sheep child *is* the vision; it *has* the vision—the world of man and beast is one world: "my father's house" is the house of us all. It is a vision before which even the sun appears momentarily to quail.

It is essential, however, not to see the sheep child only as some kind of monster-example to keep farm boys away from beasts; it is, in fact, a myth that embodies the poet's (humankind's) aspiration to union with the natural world at large. And, as Jane Bowers Martin has observed, the child is of the two worlds of nature and of art: "As a creature of memory, the sheep child, in his position with relation to the poem's narrator, transcends reality, life, in the same way that his floating existence is a transcendence of life. The sheep child is born to a world of perpetual transcendence, a world it is unnecessary to live in."[6]

Dickey likes to say, jokingly, "I don't know what other defects or virtues this poem might have, but I think it can hardly be faulted from the standpoint of originality of viewpoint" (*SI,* 165). He refers, of course, to the fact that part of the poem is told by the farm boy years later, as he recalls the proscriptive effect of the legend upon the boys' slightest sexual inclinations toward the farm animals; and to the section in which the sheep child itself, in its bottle of alcohol in the museum, speaks out. Martin, again, has made a significant observation about the split-line form of Dickey's verse, especially as it relates to the roman-type narration of the former farm boy and the italic-type narration of the sheep child:

It is the farm boy's lines that depend on these breath units, that are predominantly what Dickey calls the split line. In the sheep child's lines, however, the split line appears in only three places—the first at the description of the mating of the human and the sheep, the second at the imaginative entry of visitors to the sheep child's museum, and the third, a series of breaks, at the end of the poem, as the sheep child describes the lives the farm boys choose to lead. . . . Thus, the real world of the farm boy—where pauses for breath are necessary—is placed in juxtaposition to the transcendent world of the sheep child—where even pausing for breath is unnecessary.[7]

Of the remaining twenty-one poems in *Falling,* only one speaks from the viewpoint of animals: "Hedge Life," which drifts in the train of some of Theodore Roethke's poems ("We are small creatures, surviving / / On the one breath that grows / In our lungs in the complex green"), although several others spring out of very particular animal images. Of this group, "For the Last Wolverine" and "Encounter in the Cage Country" are the most concerned with transcendence as it is seen in "The Sheep Child."

Both are mostly confined to the "real world" and "breath" of the split line, as Martin might suggest. Both present narrators who contemplate extraordinarily energetic animals—ferocious hunters, in fact, rather than passive mythopoeic visionaries. But the poems are different in that the narrator of "For the Last Wolverine" is relatively passive himself; he imagines he instructs the extinction-bound last devil-bear to devour the heart of an elk "and, from it, have an idea / Stream into his gnawing head / That he no longer has a thing / To lose." The speaker "would" that the wolverine then climb into a tree-top, where he would meet "The New World's last eagle / Hunched in mangy feathers   giving / Up on the theory of flight." Then the wish becomes prayer: "Dear God of the wildness of poetry, let them mate / To the death in the rotten branches"; and the result of the mating springs forth fiery as a phoenix, the bird of art, specifically here the bird-beast of poetry.

The poem ends with the wolverine-eagle-beast the object of an aesthetic lesson; the narrator says, "How much the timid poem needs / / The mindless explosion of your rage," thus enforcing the sensual and purposive drive of poetry as Dickey conceives it, "to eat / The world, and not to be driven off it / Until it is gone. . . ." With such an overt proposal as to the mission of poetry, the narrator closes with a gesture to his own imagination ("I take you as you are / / And make of you what I will"); but the final lines are the imagined prayer of the carcajou itself: *"Lord, let me die   but not die / Out."* This narrative turn, giving up the human point of view at the last minute, only reiterates the clear fact that the speaker manipulates to his own inner vision the image of this dramatically powerful and persistent animal. The passionate aesthetic is strong, but it does not compare to the strength of personal identification: transcendence requires the full, if momentary, fusion of this and the not-this, humanity and the nonhuman.

"Encounter in the Cage Country" is a thoroughly dynamic poem about the transcendence possible to the Energized Man. In "For the Last Wolverine" the animal is imagined, although real before the phoenixlike apotheosis; the creature can take no active part in reaching out to the human narrator. In "Encounter in the Cage Country," as in "The Sheep Child," the worlds of nature and humankind reach toward each other; and the reaching is very special, unpredictable as it is unmistakable: "What I was would not work / For them all, for I had not caught / The lion's eye." The man in the zoo stops, stares at the black leopard, and begins—very self-consciously, in the midst of a crowd of onlookers—"To perform   first saunt'ring   then stalking / . . . faked / As if to run   and at one brilliant move / / I made as though drawing a gun. . . ." At last, after the theatrics subside, "Alert, attentive, / He waited for what I could give him." But the narrator suffers either a failure of nerve, not wanting to give "My moves   my throat   my wildest love," or a recognition that he could not forever stay locked in mystical communion with this animal. As he walks away from the encounter with the leopard, even the crowd notices a difference in him, "Quailed from me," and he recognizes a familiar-unfamiliar voice awakened with him:

> . . . I was inside and out
> Of myself   and something was given a life-
> mission to say to me hungrily over
>
> And over and over   *your moves are exactly right*
> *For a few things in this world: we know you*
> *When you come, Green Eyes, Green Eyes.*

Hidden at first behind his sunglasses, hidden then by his own flashy performance before the cage and the crowd, this man's transcendence is

almost a model of what Dickey believes is possible to all people: that when
mankind reaches out to touch the natural world in risky letting-go of
human protections, both of spirit and of body, the prospects are good that
we shall experience powers and energies that we often only dream about or
only write poems about. Poems and dreams can reveal to us, but only our
exercise of mind and affections can move us.

Falling: Transcendence Strictly Human: Power from Within

"Sun," "Adultery," and "Power and Light" all share the quality of special
energy—sensuous, dynamic, yet spiritual potency. The force is sexual, no
doubt, though the protagonist of "Power and Light" aspires to drunken
enlightenment out of a version of sexual frustration. Although "Adultery"
makes an effort to portray evenhandedly the anxious passions of the man
and the woman, all three poems are powerfully male-dominant, with
"Sun" verging on machismo sadism:

> . . . I peeled off
> Her bathing suit like her skin   her colors
> Wincing   she silently biting
> Her tongue off   her back crisscrossed with stripes
> Where winter had caught her and whipped her.

But these poems explore the pain of the male protagonists, as well. In
"Sun," the man's sunburn is as painful as his lover's; and, hot with passion
as well as their "skin crawling tighter than any / Skin of my teeth," the
two people attain together to a pinnacle of agony and delight: "Suffering
equally . . . / / As we lay, O lord, / In Hell, in love." In "Adultery," the
man and woman frequently, fearfully, check the time "to see how much /
Longer we have left," their pleasure constantly undermined and, at the
same time, heightened by the fact that "Nothing will come of us."
Whereas the lovers in "Sun" can cry painfully, ecstatically, "we are dying /
Of light   searing each other   not able / To stop   to get away," the
guiltier pair in "Adultery" tentatively affirm, "One could never die
here / / Never die   never die / While crying." In the midst of wrong-
seeming, with the tenuous but real joy of illicit union, buoyed by their
sense of somehow transcending their sordid episode and their "grim
techniques," these two urgently have sex yet one more time before they
leave. The man takes charge at the end, to be an interpreter in the midst of

this naturalistic scene: "We have done it again   we are / Still living. Sit up and smile, / God bless you. Guilt is magical."

"Power and Light" is somewhat like "The Fiend" in its depiction of the frustrated man who gains almost spiritual force, but in very physical terms, from his surroundings: as in "The Sheep Child," too, there is some suggestion of energy to be drawn for the good from nature. But most of this man's energy comes from three sources: his work, epitomized in the power and telephone lines that connect and energize him; his drinking, which loosens his inhibitions and sets him free to speak and act, at least momentarily; and—oddly enough—his home itself, including his family. It is as though neither of the other two sources could supply what is needed unless the house and his wife, particularly, are there to serve as his energizing focus. Only in facing, acting within, and then—however melodramatically inebriate—challenging his most natural place, at home, can he demonstrate his new-felt force. Almost godlike in his perception of the interconnection of all life, energy, and persons, the protagonist asserts his (perhaps temporary) truth: "I am a man / Who turns on. I am a man."

These later poems of Dickey's career move more definitely, if not decisively, into the realm of human energies. It is as though the specific pursuit of natural force has been supplanted, or at least diverted, as though the mind of the poet has seized upon the strictly human in ways that the earlier poetry only asserted in terms of the superiority of human over animal consciousness. Some of the poems in this later group are as highly charged as the best of Dickey's earlier works, but it is as though Dickey's effort to mythologize the human-nonhuman union in "The Sheep Child" was the last mighty breath, sent forth as "May Day Sermon" and "Falling," of that explicit theme. After the poems of *Falling,* external, nonhuman nature subsides dramatically in Dickey's poetry as the impetus and source of transcendent energy. With few important exceptions— "Madness" being one—Dickey's works attest to the force of the human being, specifically the force of imaginative creation.

"Falling" is Dickey's closing word in *Poems 1957–1967,* and it says plainly that human beings, all of whom are caught in a precipitous mortal plunge, can make that descent to death speak of ecstasy rather than despair. As the airline stewardess falls from high over Kansas corn fields, she is able to gain some aerodynamic mastery over her own plummeting body, to achieve some integrative vision of the diverse and fertile world beneath her, to discard the symbolic constraints of her occupational uniform ("to die / Beyond explanation"), and, in her death, with "The furrows for miles flowing in upon her where she lies very deep / In her mortal outline," to serve the American agricultural heartland as a new-found fertility goddess. She becomes herself a symbol for others. Whereas "May Day Sermon" gives us a preacher who promises to "tell" each year the story of the fugitive lovers who epitomize the "procreant urge of the world," as Walt Whitman called it, the stewardess in "Falling" preaches only two words, "Feels herself go   go toward   go outward   breathes at last fully / Not   and tries   less   once   tries   tries   AH, GOD—" Chosen to speak the last words of Dickey's first "collected poems," the stewardess utters the pure epiphany, the apotheosis of herself as goddess and the release of herself through the final human experience. She does not preach, really; in her death she quite simply becomes the sermon-object, the considered thing itself. Her downward flight through air and watery clouds, through the levels of cold and "the growing warmth / Of wheat-fields rising toward the harvest moon," through the sights of distant bus and car lights, houses and lakes, through the widest swings of joy and tragic recognition, this flight works magic on the readers as it does on the farmers, wives, and boys of the land that receives her. For Dickey, the gift of the stewardess "from the frail / Chill of space to the loam where extinction slumbers in corn tassels thickly / And breathes like rich farmers counting" is the whole human gift of sacrifice: the relinquishment of life because we are all mortal, and the simultaneous affirmation of life and meaning through the imaginative will. Few other modern American poems speak so hopefully of the universal human creative spirit.

Chapter Six
Into the Seventies

The Eye-Beaters, Blood, Victory,
Madness, Buckhead and Mercy (1970)

While *Falling* contains some of Dickey's very best poems in his "new" long-line, almost prosaic, verse, and some of those poems are startlingly fresh, even in the large context of Dickey's previous poetry, it also contains poems that might well have appeared earlier. Prefiguring "Madness" directly and *The Zodiac* more obliquely, "The Head-Aim," for example, recalls not only the human narrator's identification with nature in "Fog Envelops the Animals" but also the conjunction of vitalism and art in "Listening to Foxhounds" and "A Dog Sleeping on My Feet." Other poems in the group—"Sustainment," "Dark Ones," "Coming Back to America," and "The Birthday Dream"—are manifestly more insistent of ecstasy than the best of Dickey's work, more ponderous of intention and technique; but they do stand as appropriate foliage to the flowers of their poetic contemporaries ("The Sheep Child," "Falling," "May Day Sermon," "Power and Light"), and they do lead on. *The Eye-Beaters, Blood, Victory, Madness, Buckhead and Mercy* severely demarcates this later poetry, signified at its best by "The Eye-Beaters," "Diabetes," "Pine," "Turning Away," and "Madness," and characterized by more and more strictly human efforts through an extraordinary metaphysics of excess.

Picking up a new oratorical tone; a sometimes suspect grandiosity; a rich, associative word-flow; an incautious, occasionally monotonous but often captivating, sweeping verbal rhythm, Dickey made his first book of poems for the 1970s a thing that mostly puzzled his admirers and appalled his detractors. Even so staunch a supporter as Richard Howard fell back from saying that single poems are outstanding and chose to speak glowingly of the whole act of "poetry" that Dickey performs in *The Eye-Beaters.*[1] Other critics, who had been uneasy about the looser-lined poems in *Buckdancer's Choice* and *Falling,* abandoned ship entirely.

85

Poems Most Public.   His much-publicized feud with Robert Bly and others who considered him to be shirking his bardic responsibility to speak out during the Vietnam Era did not prevent Dickey from writing blatantly "public," even "occasional," poems. Later in his career he wrote "Exchanges" as the Phi Beta Kappa poem, Harvard University, 1970; and in 1977 he read "The Strength of Fields" at the inaugural ceremony for President Jimmy Carter. *The Eye-Beaters,* though, marks Dickey's first studiedly public poems between book covers: "In the Pocket," written for the National Football League insert to *Life* magazine, and, also for *Life,* "Apollo" (*I. For the First Manned Moon Orbit* and *II. The Ground*).

While most critics consider "In the Pocket" to be an embarrassment to the career of an excellent poet, some have admired its sense of immediacy and its unambiguous physical exuberance. In general, however, one finds it difficult to defend such diction (and typography) as, ". . . hit move scramble / Before death and the ground / Come up   LEAP STAND KILL DIE STRIKE. . . ." Even straining to make the poem a metaphor for "the game of life" does not redeem this particular kind of rhetorical excess. "The Bee," published in *Falling* and dedicated to the "coaches of Clemson College, 1942," is a football poem that operates successfully to join the past athletic experiences of the narrator with his present physical needs to save his frightened son caught amid the "murder of California traffic." To compare these two poems is to see that mere physical excitement and screaming about an experience do not make poetry.

"Apollo," unlike "In the Pocket," has a fully worthy subject, and Dickey does well with it. The poem is in two parts, each beginning with a relatively calm, meditative mood, even though the emotional tension of men traveling in space is always evident:

> So long
> So long as the void
> Is hysterical, bolted out, you float on nothing
>
> But procedure alone. . . .

Part I, "For the First Manned Moon Orbit," continues in its deliberate way, the narrator neatly concealed behind the guise of the third person, saying, "You and your computers have brought out / The silence of mountains the animal / Eye has not seen since the earth split. . . ." As the narrator-astronaut makes his turn around the moon for the first time, about to lose radio, as well as visual, contact behind the subplanet, Dickey intrudes a solid black sheet of paper in the book, representing the almost unthinkably total barrier to communication between the orbiting man and his only home in the universe, Earth. At the last second before that void, the narrator shifts to first person:

> Something I am trying
>
> [black page]
>
> To say O God
> Almighty! To come back! To complete the curve   to come back
> Singing with procedure. . . .

Such exuberance at coming back into view of the whole world is surely justified in a way that the high passion of throwing a football before getting tackled is not. And the final observation of Part I, however sentimental, is surely worth more than the game-of-life metaphor in "In the Pocket":

> And behold
>
> The blue planet steeped in its dream
>
> Of reality, its calculated vision shaking with
> The only love.

Recalling as it does Randall Jarrell's "The Death of the Ball Turret Gunner" ("Six miles from earth, loosed from its dream of life, / I woke to black flak"),[2] Dickey's poem reiterates Jarrell's sense of the solidity of earth itself, its "reality," but his obvious pleasure at the elegance of "procedure" is quite opposite to Jarrell's distaste for the modern technological warfare reported in his poem.

Part II of "Apollo," "The Moon Ground," makes it clear that the moon-landing is a team effort: "Buddy, / We have brought the gods. We know what it is to shine / Far off, with earth." The narrator wonders, even as he talks over the spacesuit intercoms, at the world of unknown knowledge that they now have small access to, and there is some fear:

> . . . will the secret crumble
> In our hands with air? Will the moon-plague kill our children
> In their beds? The Human Planet trembles in its black
> Sky with what we do   I can see it hanging in the god-gold only
> Brother of your face. We are this world: we are
> The only men. . . .

The apprehensiveness of this narrator is much less than his joy, and it is clear by the end of the poem that Dickey the poet is overcome with the excitement of the event, his imagined involvement in it as he relates to the astronauts as a former pilot himself. The imagery of the blinding gold visors on the spacehelmets lends itself to the perception of these astronauts as godlike visitors, but the earthmen are fully aware that in this most extraordinary of human missions they must "do one / Thing only, and that is rock by rock to carry the moon to take it / Back." However mundane the actual work is that they are to do, the men are exhilarated, the excess of their adventuresome spirits having cast them a quarter-million miles out of the usual course of human experience: "We stare into the moon / dust, the earth-blazing ground. We laugh, with the beautiful craze / Of static. We bend, we pick up stones." Just as Dickey had perceived in his earlier poems that the moon is yet another "ruined stone in the sky" and that it reflects and is reflected by the earth of "The only love," he sees the new, post-Apollo moon as hard rock. But now there is a huge difference.

In this public poem, he celebrates the potential for material and spiritual exploits, for growth and joy. For Dickey, at this time in his career, poetry is more exhortative, more to be pressed upon his audience, not to be left entirely to the lonely offices of private, silent readership. The mission of excess, the necessity of transcendence, is seen by the poet as something that *must* be known by everyone. The poet is more the orator than at any previous time, but his message is one of the spirit rather than of specific political or social action.

Poems Most Personal.   To call a poem "personal" is to risk entering the swamp of vague impressionism, but some qualities of the personal in Dickey's works may perhaps be agreed upon. Some poems are at least partly autobiographical. *The Eye-Beaters* opens with two two-part poems, "Diabetes" (*I. Sugar* and *II. Under Buzzards*) and "Messages" (*I. Butterflies* and *II. Giving a Son to the Sea*), which fall into this category: Dickey has referred glancingly in interviews and his own prose to having diabetes himself, and, with Chris named in "Butterflies," both parts of "Messages" appear to be addressed to his true living sons. Also, "Looking for the Buckhead Boys" (Part II of "Two Poems of Going Home") recalls the fact that Dickey was reared in the Buckhead area of Atlanta. But to pursue these correspondences is more to observe history than to clarify the personal, which is primarily a matter of tone, language, and a sense of audience.

The first seven poems of *The Eye-Beaters* are about very common subjects for sociable discourse: one's health ("Diabetes"), one's children

("Messages"), one's love-life ("Mercy"), and one's recent travels, especially "back home" ("Two Poems of Going Home"). But, as the important quality of the personal is not the autobiographical network, it is also not primarily to be found in subject matter. Rather, it is in the relationship each poem's speaker establishes with his audience by virtue of the language he uses. One might expect a poet seeking sociability to rely largely on the vernacular, since that is what the vernacular is all about—talking to most of us. And in fact several of these poems do have diction, syntax, and rhythms that spring from our most common speech. But to accomplish a personal poem such as Dickey manages in "Sugar" is more than to deliberate, "wondering what / The hell"; to assent with "O.K."; to exclaim (with some reserve), "Not bad!"; to confide, "My weight is down"; or to say almost offhandedly, "Really it is better / To know when to die."

What Dickey does, and not always successfully, is to risk an easily parsed consistency in order to achieve a very particular narrative voice, that of an educated man whose passions are common enough to be perceived by ordinary people and whose expression in language is colorful but not exotic, engaging but forceful, and entertaining but not condescending. These poems have an air of performance about them, not like Donald Armstrong's, or the narrator's in "Encounter in the Cage Country," exactly, but with elements of that self-consciousness. Dickey's performances here are like those of a good storyteller with his friends; they require some gift from the reader, a suspension of distrust, a willingness to tolerate the boisterous swells of hyperbole, the rifts among various levels of diction and imagery, and the occasionally blatant sentimentality, all to the end of tapping a source of whole-life energy. These poems are not introspective-personal; they are, shall we say, public-personal. They want an audience not just to overhear what they say but also to participate in the conversation. The subjects are considered everybody's; the mood, expansive and inclusive.

Many—perhaps most—of Dickey's earlier poems are dramatically structured; that is, they involve someone else present and to some extent interactive with the narrator. Sometimes it is friends ("Listening to Foxhounds"), family members ("The String"), a woman ("Coming Back to America"), ghostly spirits ("The Underground Stream," "Drinking from a Helmet"), or even variant ecstasies of the narrator himself ("The Other"). Very few, however, depend for their important structures largely upon the narrator's directly addressing, or conversing with, the other figure in the drama.

"Sugar" and "Under Buzzards" make references to "friend," "companion," and "brother," all of which could as well refer to the narrator's own
other selves, an internal and self-cast dramatic production; but the tone of
"Sugar," at least, and its quotation of the narrator's dialogue with his
doctor suggest that this could be a story told to a very sympathetic listener,
face to face:

> . . . The doctor was young
>
> And nice. He said, I must tell you,
> My friend, that it is needles moderation
> And exercise. You don't want to look forward
> To gangrene and kidney
>
> Failure   boils blindness infection skin trouble falling
> Teeth coma and death.
>   O.K. . . .

Some passages, like "Moderation, moderation, / My friend, and exercise,"
indicate the narrator's reluctant acquiescence to the medical regimen, and
the development of the sugar imagery—"Gangrene in white" becomes
"the real / Symbol of Time I could eat / And live with"—conveys the
"friend's" growing trust in the narrator's story and his complicity, though
silent, in the elaborating verbal texture.

"Under Buzzards" might more readily be seen as an internal drama,
with the narrator talking intensely to himself about the gathering "birds of
death." He refers in line one to a "Companion" who shares his mortal
plight: "We are level / Exactly on this moment." As the poem progresses,
the diabetic fever, the insulin rush, and the beer-drinking against all
conventional advice drive the narrator inward upon his own feelings, but
the "brother" attends to the end. As the narrator drifts to the second-
person "You know," he finally asks a favor:

> . . . Companion, open that beer.
> How the body works   how hard it works
>   For its medical books is not
>   Everything: everything is how
>   Much glory is in it. . . .

And thus the brother assists in an actual, or a psychodramatic, suicide
through diabetic imbalance. The narrator has spent his last energies

socializing (perhaps with himself) and drinking beer to his mortal detriment. The desire for the "glorious movement" of the buzzards has allowed the narrator to trade moderation and years for excess and ecstasy: ". . . my body is turning   is flashing unbalanced / Sweetness everywhere, and I am calling my birds."

Both "Butterflies" and "Giving a Son to the Sea" are directly addressed to the poet's sons, Chris and (although he is unnamed in the poem) Kevin. But these are not direct addresses, like Jack Lemmon's in the film *Tribute,* in which the words ostensibly spoken to the son are also—and perhaps primarily—for the listening audience. To Chris, Dickey asserts the continuing pleasures of play, for both father and son. But the confidential tone (reminiscent of "To His Children in Darkness") spills abundantly outward. The poet plays with the skeleton of a cow, pulling at the horns and scrutinizing "inside the nose-place . . . packets / And whole undealt decks / Of thin bones, like shaved playing cards." The son lies asleep in no imminent danger atop the grassy earth dam, "holding back / Water without strain." There, with the intensity of changes, the pressures of natural forces upon the momentary joys of people, the poet-father speaks public-personally to the son, sleeping then, but now awake to the poem, and to the whole audience around.

To Kevin, the son who at six fired the secret-message bullet with "I love you" to his father, the poet speaks gently; for the son is gentle, and the threat he is under is serious. This son does not rest under butterflies above the straining water and near the death-carriage skeleton his father exercises; Kevin is a deep swimmer in the sea. The father tells him of the world's expectations ("someone must lead / Mankind"), but mostly this son is already committed, it seems, to his dangerous public task.

In some ways, "Mercy" is more complex in its dramatic narration than either "Diabetes" or "Messages." Somewhat reminiscent of Eliot's "The Love Song of J. Alfred Prufrock," "Mercy" opens with the narrator walking at night to meet an appointment with a woman (Prufrock is much less direct, as he seems to be moving toward a vaguely defined social engagement at which women are present). Dickey's narrator is accompanied by some vaguely defined companion known only—and swiftly, in one word—as "we." Not so fastidious as Prufrock, Dickey's narrator is nonetheless concerned with his clothing's appearance, and he is inclined to what seem to be questions addressed to his walking companion but which might just as well be rhetorical, addressed only to himself and the poem's audience. And his path, like Prufrock's, leads into oblique and circuitous ways. Dickey's narrator gives his reader the direct and indirect dialogue

with the housemother, other nurses, and Fay herself as he sees his date the
first time this night, as he takes her explanation for tardiness (being in the
operating room), and as he waits—again engaging in conversation with
housemother and others—for Fay to descend after her shower and the brief
delay of her dressing. As with "Diabetes," this narrator seems to be
speaking at various times with himself, his audience, and his characters
within the poem. But throughout, the poet is manipulating the reader's
expectations and sense that they—the audience—are in on the narrator's
best efforts to reproduce for a sympathetic listener the experience of
waiting for and being rewarded by the presence of the narrator's "Fay . . .
you big cow-bodied / Love o yes." Unlike Eliot, whose Prufrock has little
interest in securing the reader's sense of time and time-passage, Dickey's
narrator tells outright when he shifts into some mode other than the
immediate narrative:

> . . . She's been married; her aunt's
> Keeping the kids. I reckon you know that, though. I do,
> And I say outside
> Of time, there must be some way she can strip
> Blood off. . . .

As the narrator concedes that he knows Fay's circumstances, his passion
leads him to imagine "outside / Of time" that she could do something to
hasten her preparation to be with him after her bloody encounter in the
operating room.

"Mercy" shifts radically in its narrative emphasis, however, until in the
final lines it is almost entirely—and hyperbolically—addressed to Fay
herself, who becomes by the conclusion "O queen of death / Alive, and
with me at the end." As Dickey's narrator has progressed through his
personal experience of approach, anticipation, social chit-chat, and his
long-awaited actual lovemaking with Fay, the voice becomes more and
more complex, more and more personal, even as the speaker has actively
engaged his companion-audience. The poetic situations and their
metaphysical correspondences are fairly blunt—mortality as the adjunct to
the hospital and nurses' home; the name of the manor itself, Mercy, as a
sign of the saving grace of the place and the women in it; the final
association of the woman-mother-nurse Fay as the queen of death who shall
save the narrator's life. But the true accomplishment of this poem is in its
masterful blending of the actual, the fantasy, the inner thoughts, and the

outer dialogue, of the narrator, for whom the physical presence of Nurse Fay in their actual lovemaking is enough to energize and to transform him from the self-conscious, clothes-questioning suitor to the man who rumbles at the boundaries of death and finds in his woman some ecstatic new life.

"Living There," Part I of "Two Poems of Going Home," and "Looking for the Buckhead Boys," Part II, are each quite different from the other; but, taken together, their narrative voice proceeds in a clear progression from introspective, metaphysical, and relatively tense to much looser, more sociable recollection of the good-ol'-boy days of high-school places and friends. "Living There" opens with a very solemn third-person mystery: "The Keeper / Is silent   is living in the air not / Breathable, of time." In line nine, the narrator indicates that this poem is all internalized, with himself talking—but mostly thinking—to himself: "Old Self like a younger brother, like a son, we'd come rambling / Out of the house in wagons. . . ." Later, he speaks of this self-within-self as "you and I, / My youth and my middle / Age. . . ." As the poem evolves, it becomes plain that the narrator is himself the Keeper, that his past, its places and its people, its events and its most subtle feelings, are only to be maintained by his own active memory. The burden is enormous, but finally the speaker reveals—somewhat melodramatically and sentimentally—that some of the keeping is accomplished through his sons.

"Looking for the Buckhead Boys" tries to do some of the things with interior and exterior dialogue that "Mercy" accomplishes. The narrator begins as though he were cheerleading himself to locate the old friends of his youth, but he begins with too strong a metaphor, claiming blindness as the cause of his inability to find his old haunts. The rest of the poem suffers also from a kind of overkill. Thinking of the Buckhead Boys, the narrator says,

> . . . If I can find them, even one,
> I'm home. And if I can find him   catch him in or around
> Buckhead, I'll never die: it's likely my youth will walk
> Inside me like a king.

Such overstatement, especially as it comes at the beginning of the poem, before the poet has had time to engage his audience to such extreme responses, only serves to heighten the suspicion that this talk is mostly blather and very little poetry. This is not to deny the cleverness and humor, even some of the pathos, of the poem, but "Looking for the Buckhead Boys" is evidence of the dead-end outer limits of the sociable-discourse poem of this period of Dickey's career.

Most noteworthy in Dickey's public-personal mode is his effort to test the limits of his language and his themes. In his strong turn away from the elitist modernism of Eliot and Pound, Dickey has wanted to make poetry touch more people. He has felt that mission somewhat as Walt Whitman claimed to have. In his pursuit of that egalitarian goal, in his desire—like Wordsworth's—to find regeneration in the passionate speech of the common man, Dickey has stretched his poetic language drastically in the direction of the vernacular, the exclamatory, the prosaic. His willingness to explore, in "The Cancer Match," "Venom," and "Blood," the extremities of disease and alcohol, poison, sexuality, including—in the curious fantasia of "Victory"—homosexuality, allows his readers access to an astonishing range of emotions, all calculated poetically to lift jaded humanity out of the dull and familiar to more intense, even transcendent, experiences.

Toward "The Star-beasts of Intellect and Madness."   Some of the poems in *The Eye-Beaters* press for more intense, rather than radical or excessive, enlightenment. "The Place," with its exquisite sense of pain and isolation; "Knock," with its hesitant fearfulness; and "The Lord in the Air," with its similarities to earlier poems about calling the natural creatures, summoning them to human will, in this case the poet's son's will—all these are unexceptional works.

Two other poems are more purely rhythmic and mellifluous, as well as imagistically sensuous. "Pine," called, as in an epigraph, "successive apprehensions," is couched in terms so as almost to obliterate any human narrator. The poem accomplishes what "Springer Mountain" and "Rein-carnation (II)" both aspire to, the sensuous, almost entirely nonrational apprehensions of the natural world. Like the blind child in "The Owl King," the narrator of "Pine" restructures sense-impressions synaesthetically, as though these physical expressions of nature had never been gathered or held before: "So any hard hold / Now loses; form breathes near." Like A. R. Ammons's "Corsons Inlet," Dickey's poem tends to blur the usual rational discriminations that people make and then use to restrict their own lives. "Pine" is a momentary setting-free of the creative mind amid the sensuous elements of nature; there, as the narrator exults in conclusion,

> . . . A final form
> And color at last comes out
> Of you alone putting it all
> Together like nothing
> Here like almighty
>
> V
>
> Glory.

"Turning Away," subtitled "Variations on Estrangement," does not so much glory in the human capacity for wise assimilation and creation. Rather, it meditates with close reason and painful emotions on the ramifications of estrangement as it may take place between two people and within oneself. Drawing upon the imagery of kings and sons, battlefields and peaceful meadows, past and present that made "Dover: Believing in Kings" a work of hope and rich potentiality, this poem captures the breath-tight constrictions of broken communion:

> Turning away, the eyes do not mist over
> Despite the alien sobbing in the room.
> Withhold! Withhold! Stand by this window
>
> As on guard
> Duty   rehearsing what you will answer
> If questioned. . . .

The intensity and aural beauty of "Pine" and "Turning Away," however, are not typical of Dickey's work in general. They are more like musical tone-poems, the complex subtleties of chamber orchestra, or even string quartet, rather than the bluntly melodic ballad or the vigorously dramatic ballet. The usual thing for Dickey is to strive for energy rather than beauty. In the concluding lines of *The Zodiac,* Dickey's narrator declares that poetry shall "Make what it can of what is: / / So long as the spirit hurls on space / The star-beasts of intellect and madness." Although they do not deal in zodiacal, heavenly terms, both "Madness" and "The Eye-Beaters" work toward that creative mission.

"Madness" is narrated through the consciousness of a domestic dog who seeks springtime relief for his sexual urges: "Help me was shouted / To the

world of females. . . ." He is bitten by a rabid vixen; in turn he bites a
child of his own household, after which he is killed and beheaded. The
poem is marvelously coherent in its rhythmic movement, as it is tautly
expressive of Dickey's views of sexuality, springtime, and excess as modes
of knowledge and creativity. Even though the madness leads to the dog's
death, he has seen the edges of existence. Like the sheep child he speaks to
the human world which fears his madness as it fears the sheep child's
monstrosity—its message is one of purest transcendence, of absolutely
intensified mortal experience, up to and over the boundaries of death. At
the end of "The Birthday Dream," in which the narrator suffers a nightmare of four men "looking for somebody / To beat up," the dreamer
awakes to discover that "The room was full of mildness. I was forty." At
the conclusion of "Madness," the narrative voice—now in and now out of
the mind of the beheaded dog—refers to another kind of mildness:

> . . . this was something
>
> In Spring in mild brown eyes   as strangers
>   Cut off the head and carried and held it
>   Up, blazing with consequence   blazing
>   With freedom saying   bringing
>   Help   help   madness   help.

For Dickey, madness—even as it leads to death—is preferable to a life that
lacks intensity and "consequence." Early in the poem, the dog calls for
help from "the world of females"; at the end, he "says" and "brings" help
through the example of his own sudden enlightenment.

If not the best—and it is very good—"The Eye-Beaters" is surely the
most important poem in this volume. Its premise is bizarre; its execution,
experimental; its process, archetypal; and its blunt optimism at the end,
almost Victorian. Other poems in *The Eye-Beaters* explore the extremities
of disease, drunkenness, violence, estrangement, and madness; but this
poem comes closest, perhaps, to fulfilling the double poetic function of
"intellect and madness." Its premise is that blind children who beat their
eyes can achieve a sensation that is somewhat like sight. The dramatic
situation is indicated in the first of the marginalia of the poem (a technique
recalling "The Rime of the Ancient Mariner," by Coleridge): "*A man visits
a Home for children in Indiana, some of whom have gone blind there.*" The man
encounters a therapist, who explains some of the children's experiences,
and he also begins to consider what sights and motives the children might

have. Their predicament is so unsettling to him that *"The Visitor begins to invent a fiction to save his mind,"* a fiction in which he imagines that the visions of troubled children reach back into the racial memory, offering modern persons access to the earliest images of art—cave drawings—and (among) the earliest impulses of human behavior—hunting. The narrative voice moves through interior and exterior monologue, including exchanges with the therapist and, most peculiarly, exchanges between the Visitor's Reason and his Invention. The implication of this radical technique is that meaningful action, a life "blazing with consequence," can be generated only by a synthesis of rational and irrational capacities within human beings. The man who views the eye-beaters must make some kind of peace for himself between the ideal condition of these children—fully able to see—and the actual—blind. The resolution is effected through the imagination of the Visitor as he projects rich and primordial apprehensions upon the struggling children.

Finally, of course, the projections can only serve him and, as he is a poet, his readers; they cannot help the children at the moment. Their hard condition is too nearly unbearable: "No; / by god. There is no help for this but madness, / Perversity." The children are perverse for their self-abuse; God is perverse for allowing them to be blind; and the Visitor is perverse for his fully conscious act of imagining some more glorious visions for them than they can know. Perversity, often relating to physical violence, recurs throughout Dickey's work, especially in the later poems and *Deliverance*; but, unlike "The Fiend," "Blood," "Victory," "The Sheep Child," "Sun," "May Day Sermon," and "Falling," this poem—"The Eye-Beaters"—allows a complete transcendence of the particular violent acts and culminates in the sanguine commitment of the Visitor to go forth intensified and energized: ". . . I merge, I pass beyond in secret   in perversity and the sheer / Despair of invention   my double-clear bifocals off   my reason gone / Like eyes. Therapist, farewell at the living end. Give me my spear." Having exercised his reason thoroughly in trying to comprehend the children's experience, having debated within the forum of himself, the Visitor can now go into his life again with the confidence of instinct, the training of the hunter, the athlete of the imagination.

The Zodiac (1976)

Robert Penn Warren declared *The Zodiac* "a major . . . achievement"[3] when it first appeared in print. In *Poetry,* Dave Smith called it "important as an impressive failure and as a transitional poem for Dickey."[4] Stopping just short of charging plagiarism, however, some others have found that his disclaimer in the book is not adequate to disguise and vindicate the insufficiency of his paraphrase, imitation, or rewrite of a poem that he knew from A. J. Barnouw's translation from the *Sewanee Review*—Dutch poet Hendrik Marsman's "The Zodiac."[5] Dickey acknowledges: "This poem is based on another of the same title. It was written by Hendrik Marsman, who was killed by a torpedo in the North Atlantic in 1940. It is in no sense a translation, for the liberties I have taken with Marsman's original poem are such that the poem I publish here, with the exception of a few lines, is completely my own." Almost all of Dickey's critics have either dismissed or so qualified their acceptance of *The Zodiac* that it floats in space, ungrounded and untended by "received opinion," waiting for oblivion or some hearty defense.

The Zodiac's story, a painful, sometimes raucous one, is endangered as a seriously regarded object of literary criticism perhaps because of a minor error in its being printed in a book with short, wide pages, giving the appearance of a children's book, but more harmfully suggesting that it can be read quickly to the sound of ruffling leaves. More importantly, it may be disregarded for its narrator's being called a Dutch poet when he is obviously an American, with American speech patterns and the plainest influences of "The Waste Land" upon it.

Dickey indicates in a preliminary note that "Its twelve sections are the story of a drunken and perhaps dying Dutch poet who returns to his home in Amsterdam after years of travel and tries desperately to relate himself, by means of stars, to the universe." In a vigorous, sympathetic review, "The Strength of James Dickey," Dave Smith designates some of the major thematic and formal concerns of *The Zodiac:*

Organized in twelve zodical [*sic*] and seasonal panels, occurring within twenty-four hours, and being an approximation of the dying poet's mind-flow mediated through Dickey, with intrusive commentary by Dickey, *The Zodiac* is not a narrative progression except as the poet-hero's madness implies the eternal story of "connecting and joining things that lay their meanings / Over billions of light years," or the madness of failure and fear. Nature, in *The Zodiac*, is either the meaning of stars or their deadness. Dickey's oscillating journey, in the poet's "story," is now between the failure of everything on earth (history, time, love, home—all betrayals) and whatever, if anything, stars are saying. In this sense, *The Zodiac* is entirely self-referential and everything to which the poet responds leaves him aware he is only a prisoner of illusion. Darkness reigns.[6]

Despite its general good will and, unfortunately, because of its perpetuation of the idea that the poem has no narrative movement, Smith's review does not much help the reputation of *The Zodiac,* which is not nearly so "transitional" as it is a culmination of Dickey's theme of transcendence and his long development of a very American postmodernist narrator. At the simplest level of definition, one may see the Zodiac-poet as a protagonist who has a goal at the beginning of the poem, who sets about to attain that goal, and who, through various trials and obstructions, comes to some demonstrable success or resolution. What Smith calls mere "oscillating" is in fact Dickey's exercise upon the classical unities of time, place, and action: the poet, in twenty-four hours in his own home town of Amsterdam, works "desperately to relate himself . . . to the universe." A grandiose scheme, no doubt, but clearly partaking of the elements of plot.

Discovered at the beginning in a miserable state of depression and drunkenness, the poet settles upon a plan to engage cosmic meaning through a willful imaginative act upon the heavenly order, the zodiac—the defining event. As he goes through various efforts, both purposely and uncontrollably, he imagines and hallucinates to such an extent that his own created Lobster descends, under orders from a much-offended God, to claw him to death—the crisis. The DTs over, and exhausted, the poet is able momentarily to rest from his active contemplation of Time, Eternity, and his own poor plight. In Section VI, a short dream sequence, the denouement is evidently underway. He works out his understanding that the whole knowledge he has sought is not to be commanded by reason: "one part of his brain goes soft . . . but the spirit turns to fire." With some hint of resolution overriding the dispirited resignation that one might expect, the poet begins to gather force: "The sweat of thought breaks out." He speaks, still cynically, but with a change in emphasis from abstract metaphysics to concrete love, as he suffers the fever of his exertion: "It crowns him like a fungus: / Idea of love / *Love?* / Yes, but who'll put a washrag on him?"

Section VII opens with the poet still trying to get himself "back in shape," but the new poetic line-forms he uses in this section confirm his rising energy and his clearing mind:

> He says from his terrible star-sleep,
> Don't shack up with the intellect:
> Don't put your prick in a cold womb.
> Nothing but walking snakes would come of *that*—

> But if you conceive with meat
>
> Alone,
>   that child, too, is doomed.

As the lines become more brusque, even ferocious in their assertions, the poet grows more confident in his final urge to meaning—through poetry, black lines, the darkness upon the stark and blinding white page.

In Section VII, the poet decides, "Leave it, and get out. Go back to the life of a man." And Section VIII marks his efforts to that end. He remembers his mother, his father (who was himself an "astronomer / Of sorts"), his own youth, his early but despised girlfriend ("the little bitch who filled, with *his* hand, / His diary with dreadful verses"). In Section X he makes love but recognizes that "he knows that nothing, / Even love, can kill off his lonesomeness." He visits a friend, observes and discusses art, food, women, politics, postcards, and music—accordion music.

Finally, in Section XII, after "A day like that," the poet finds himself in his room, facing the "face-up flash" of the page awaiting his poetry:

> . . . He crouches bestially,
> The darkness stretched out on the waters
> Pulls back, humming Genesis. From wave-stars lifts
> A single island wild with sunlight,
> The white sheet of paper in the room.

His godlike aspirations are not hopeless, even though, as he writes, "The virgin sheet becomes / More and more his, more and more another mistake." Contrary to what Smith says, Dickey's poet-narrator does not submit to "the failure of everything on earth"; for him, poetry offers great value—not perfect, surely, but great. In Section I he knows that reason is not enough: "The Zodiac. / He must solve it   must believe it   learn to read it / No, wallow in it / As poetry." Even at his most despairing, when he denies knowing "a damn thing of stars   of God   of space. . . ," he withholds the final disavowal, saying, "*Not much* of poetry" (emphasis ours). He recognizes the deadening effect of the too-personal on art: ". . . he can't get rid of himself enough / To write poetry." And, in that same desperate opening Section I, he comes to a serious image of writing that persists to the end of the poem:

> The secret is that on whiteness you can release
> The blackness,
>   The night sky. Whiteness is death   is dying
>   For human words to raise it from purity   from the grave
>   Of too much light. Words must come to it
> Words from *any*where. . . .

And this poem does take its words from anywhere, for its mission is to find some kind of imaginative, synthesizing truth where "the stars and his balls meet," something cosmic and close, "far out and far in": "Look, stupid, get your nose out of the sky for once. / There're things that are *close* to you, too. Look at *that!* / Don't cringe: look right out over town."

In the final Section, XII, the poet acknowledges that his is a "defeated body," but he speaks to his soul, asking power for his writing hand: "Oh my own soul, put me in a solar boat. / Come into one of these hands / Bringing quietness and . . . rare belief." He appears not broken but restructured, not darkly despairing but wisely resolved that his art-effort, the poetry of his life, may have consequence, but only

> So long as the hand can hold its island
>   Of blazing paper, and bleed for its images:
>   Make what it can of what is:
>
>   So long as the spirit hurls on space
>   The star-beasts of intellect and madness.

Poetic Recapitulation in "The New Life"

After *The Zodiac* (1976), Dickey published *Tucky the Hunter* in 1978, a book-length children's poem about Dickey's grandson, James Bayard Tuckerman Dickey (son of Chris), who imagines in his bed at night that he shoots all sorts of wild animals, birds, and even angels with his pop-gun. The poem is rimed, jingly, sometimes surprising, often amusing, and very successful at public readings. The familiar theme of hunting and spiritual exchange with nature is evident: "They sang in mystic double-tongue, the tongue of man and beast." Even the recurrent presence of the suburbs in Dickey's work is recalled. Given its limited terms, *Tucky the Hunter* seems to work.

In 1979, with the publication of *The Strength of Fields* Dickey gathered the poems of *Head-Deep in Strange Sounds: Free-Flight Improvisations from the unEnglish* (a luxury edition from Palaemon Press, also 1979, of loose translations, imitations, and rewrites) and appended them to thirteen other poems, to which he owed no unEnglish debt. Of these thirteen, three were first published in 1969, two in 1970, two (plus three "translations" from Yevtushenko, the Russian poet) in 1971, one in 1972, two in 1973, and one ("For the Running of the New York City Marathon") bears no acknowledgment as to its prior publication at all. This is to say that only two of the wholly original poems in this first Dickey collection since *The Eye-Beaters,* almost a decade before, were less than six years old. And one of them, although generally superior to the genre, is an "occasional" poem: "The Strength of Fields," written for President Jimmy Carter and read by the poet at the inaugural ceremony on national television in 1977. It is no secret that, for whatever personal and professional reasons, Dickey spent most of the 1970s not writing poems but shifting his energies to *Deliverance* (book and movie), the screenplay for *The Call of the Wild* (a TV movie of Jack London's novel), the lavish books, *Jericho* and *God's Images,* other motion-picture projects, some essays, and a long-term novel-in-progress, *Alnilam* (newly entitled *A Minor Constellation,* in an *Esquire* attribution).[7]

The Strength of Fields is dedicated to his second wife, "To Deborah / in the new life," but whereas *The Zodiac* is a culmination of the techniques and aesthetic theories of Dickey up to 1976, *The Strength of Fields* is mostly just a collection—a good one, but not particularly fresh. It is not in itself the sign of "the new life"; rather, it is a gathering of forces, the recapitulation of strengths of this poet, and that makes it very much worth reading.

Except for "Exchanges," there are, surprisingly, no love poems in the first part of the book, and the woman in that poem is but one of several major imagistic threads. One sexual-memory fantasy, "Root-light, or the Lawyer's Daughter," is reported through the relatively innocent eyes of an eight-year-old. Granted, the poem is written by the full-grown male poet, but the effective image is less that of overt sexuality and more of an astonishingly sensual moment when a boy forms an ineradicable woman-ideal that he had no way to prepare for. The poem is taut, short, and brilliant as an opener to the volume.

The only other poem in which a woman is prominent is "The Voyage of the Needle," and the woman is the boy's mother, who taught him to float a needle upon the surface-tension of his bath. Published perhaps incongruously in *Gentleman's Quarterly,*[8] the poem is as taut as "Root-light," but, with the floating needle above the submerged naked body of the boy bathing, its sexual overtones are much more oblique. The narrator calls the phenomenon "that magic, like a mother's spell / Cast in sharp seed in your childhood, in scientific trickery rooted / And flowering in elation." Then he speaks almost sentimentally of a woman's giving birth, the fragility of any child's life, and the delicacy of relationships between family members, especially of opposite sex.

It is somewhat ironic that a volume whose title poem tells a new President that the chief virtue is "kindness" and that it "will do nothing less / Than save" us all should follow that poem immediately with "Two Poems of the Military." But the first, "Haunting the Maneuvers," deals somewhat humorously with war games in Louisiana, in which flour sacks explode "death / White" to mark the losers in the competition; and the second, "Drums Where I Live," describes the narrator's occasional unease at the sounds of a military base near his home, with the question and answer about war, ". . . where in God's / Name did it start? In peace, two, three, four: / In peace peace peace peace. . . ." Of "Two Poems of Flight-Sleep," the first, "Camden Town," speaks very sensitively of the young pilot-in-training who finds himself in what he calls "Death's baby machine," wanting at times to escape, even into sleep in flight and ultimately to death. The second of this group, "Reunioning Dialogue," is in the too-casual language of "Looking for the Buckhead Boys." But this poem strains even beyond that other strained poem and lacks its humor.

Sports poems tend to be humorless, too; and "For the Death of [Vince] Lombardi" is no exception, although Dickey is obviously working hard to elevate the legendary coach's personal struggle against cancer, his career of the winning philosophy, and at the same time trying to use but alter the pervasive cliches of football. If Dickey had written only "In the Pocket" and this, "Lombardi" would have benefited greatly by comparison; but we do have "The Bee," a football poem with passionate physicality, a warm heart, and a clear head. "Lombardi" cannot match that combination. "For the Running of the New York City Marathon," despite its efforts at humor, fares even less well.

Four excellent poems in *The Strength of Fields* recapitulate various degrees of the public and personal voices Dickey developed in the late 1960s. It is probably only coincidental, but they progress chronologically from more public to more personal. "Exchanges" is the second truly "occasional" poem in this book. Written as the Phi Beta Kappa poem, Harvard University, 1970, it is also the most truly experimental, "being," as the epigraph says, "in the form of a dead-living dialogue with Joseph Trumbull Stickney (1874–1904)." Intermingling quotations from Stickney's poems with his own lines, Dickey explores with remarkable unity his love for a now-dead young woman, whom he remembers with him and his guitar atop an ocean-side California cliff; the ecological furor over whale-deaths, smog, and oil companies; the inhuman, deathless, dead surface of the moon; and then the connection of humanity with the moon by rocket-travel. The main point of the poem takes the form of a public pronouncement, a secular prayer:

> O astronauts,
> Poets, all those
> *Of the line of wizards and saviors,* spend your lives
> And billions of dollars to show me
> The small true world
> Of death, the place we sang to
> From Zuma. . . .

"False Youth: Autumn: Clothes of the Age" (1971), a distinctive companion to, but much funnier than, "False Youth: Two Seasons," in *Falling,* has the air of public performance conspicuous in "Encounter in the Cage Country"; but here there is no animal—except as the poet himself comes to represent one to the audience of the "redneck" barber shop. The tone is casual and decidedly humorous:

> Three red foxes on my head, come down
> There last Christmas from Brooks Brothers
> As a joke, I wander down Harden Street
> In Columbia, South Carolina, fur-haired and bald. . . .

As he is in the chair, the waiting customers comment, "Jesus, if there's anything I hate / It's a middle-aged hippie"; "When're you gonna put on that hat, / Buddy?"; and finally, "Goodbye, Fox." But before he leaves, the narrator theatrically dons his embroidered denim jacket, on which "the mother of my grandson" has formed an eagle with a flag, now "Disintegrating":

> . . . I stop with my fox
> Head at the glass to let the row of chairs spell it out
> And get a lifetime look at my bird's
> One word, raggedly blazing with extinction and soaring loose
> In red threads burning up white until I am shot in the back
> Through my wings   or ripped apart
> For rags:
> *Poetry.*

"The Rain Guitar" (1972) is located in England, 1962, with the narrator watching submerged water-grass in motion and idly observing "that flow is forever / Sealed from rain in a weir." Two images, of his guitar and his sweater, are heightened for him by the fact that it is raining, and he wonders if it is that guitars are improved or deteriorated by moisture; at the same time he is very conscious of the thirsty fabric of his sweater drinking in the rain. Unlike "False Youth: Autumn," in which the narrator is on stage before an essentially detached comic audience, "The Rain Guitar" portrays the narrator's encounter with a wartime veteran who has lost his leg; the poet has an audience in his little poetic drama, but the response he has is warmly personal, not theatrical:

> . . . I was Air Force,
> I said, So was I; I picked
> This up in Burma, he said, tapping his gone leg
> With his fly rod, as Burma and the South
> west Pacific and North Georgia reeled,
> Rapped, cast, chimed, darkened and drew down
> Cathedral water, and improved.

Such a restrained but rich conclusion indicates the compression of memory, external fact and internal truth.

Most internalized of all these poems is "Remnant Water" (1973), in which the narrator, probably an American Indian, stands alone contemplating a dying body of water, a lake or pond whose fish life and plant life are subject to "scum-gruel . . . In ruination's suck-holing acre." The language is severe and guttural; spoken aloud in a public-meeting tirade against the social or natural forces that produce such desiccation and slime, they would seem excessive. But as they are the unspoken, interior monologue of this man "Alone, in my tribal sweat   my people gone my fish rolling / Beneath me," the passionate thoughts of the affected insider rather than the abstractly concerned outsider, the severe diction feels appropriate, personal.

As Dave Smith says of the second part of *The Strength of Fields,* "Head-Deep in Strange Sounds: Free-Flight Improvisations from the unEnglish," "All continue Dickey's theme of the heroic Energized Man, but all are, in style, radically discontinuous with Dickey's characteristic work. They are short, terse, and intensely imagistic of body though written mostly in long, gap-punctuated and spatially dispersed lines. There was always a surreal quality to Dickey's poetry, and it is strong here."[9] Perhaps it is also true that these poems are notable for a quality of holding back; in "Mexican Valley," the word "gone" occurs as an initial-position adjective ("my gone sight") as it does in "The Rain Guitar" ("his gone leg") and "Remnant Water" ("the gone depths"). They thus convey much lostness, much unsayableness: "I am tired of existing / As an animal of intelligence— / Don't try to name what is nameless" ("Low Voice, Out Loud," Léon-Paul Fargue). Smith sees *The Zodiac* as a poetic relative to these foreign-tongued poems, in style and content; but one might argue that the "Three Poems with Yevtushenko," with their exclamatory fatigue ("I'm tired of killing. I'm not a damn thing but old"), published in 1971, were for Dickey precursors to the soul-weariness of the Marsman imitation. Also, other Dickey poems prefigure the hesitation, suspension, and elusiveness of the most recent of these "Free-Flights": "Dark Ones," "The Flash," "The Place," "Knock," and perhaps some of the mystico-mythic poems of *Into the Stone*. At any rate, it is safe to say that these poems represent a further drawing back from the position of the public orator, a turning inward and intensifying of the poet.

This effort at introspection and subtilizing has produced an extraordinary *tour de force* in *Puella,* published in 1982 and also dedicated to Deborah, *"her girlhood, male-imagined."* These poems about the growth of a girl into young womanhood are partly an exercise in language—particularly with participles—as it tries to *be* in some way the thing it represents. In this, the experiment recalls Gerard Manley Hopkins, whom Dickey cites in the epigraph to "Heraldic: Deborah and Horse in Morning Forest." Some techniques for which Hopkins is well known are here Dickey's: the compounding of unusual words; the reliance upon fragmentary images—sometimes single words—for the effect of simultaneity; the expectation that readers will follow attentively into unfamiliar language patterns, syntax, oddly musical tones, in order to perceive with the poet some new and unknowable—except in these new terms—sense of what the world is like; and—less a technique than a metaphysical shift—a movement toward the transcendent world of blended cosmos, the world beyond the stars (beyond *The Zodiac*), the world in which all the idiosyncrasies of individuals and of the aberrent nature we live in are subsumed. Dickey strikes an Emersonian gong as he speaks of "The whole mingling oversouling loom / Of this generation. . . ." It is more like Eliot's world "above the moving tree" ("Burnt Norton," 1. 58), and more like Hopkins's God-view world than we should have thought Dickey would have come to, even late in his life.

At age fifty-nine, then, with this slim volume obviously on-line for a Collected Poems of James Dickey, perhaps to celebrate his sixtieth year in

1983, Dickey has stepped somewhat away from the modes of reader-accessibility that gave him an enthusiastic popular audience but that also led him to the brink of banality in the 1970s; in *Puella* the poet expects his readers to *do* something, to work more for what they get.

Aside from whether or not he actually attains to the inner mind of a young woman, the Dickey messages are still much the same. He espouses energy, high-spiritedness, blood-consciousness, "terror and control," sexual potency (if not necessarily fertility), all the familiar themes. But this new feeling of Otherness is not the impending and dangerous creatureliness of the night and of the dark muscles and fluids of the body that we have seen with such astonishment in the past twenty-five years of Dickey's work. Rather, here he has extended himself into the "wide-open collisionless color of the whole night / Ringed-in, pure surface." It is true, of course, that when his Deborah-narrator holds her mirror in her right hand and sees herself, the moon, and the implicit sun in its "blocked-back shimmer," the woman comes to feel some vibrant mystery that both is and is not herself: "A woman's live playing of the universe / As inner light, stands clear, / And is, where I last was." But it is also true that these poems were written by a man in his middle and late fifties, whose other poems about women have tended toward either idealization or male domination. The epigraph to the book is from T. Sturge Moore, and its thesis clearly indicates that the former impulse, to imagine an inspiring woman through some sort of dream and then to seek an embodiment of that ideal, informs this intriguing sixth-decade project of James Dickey: "I lived in thee, and dreamed, and waked / Twice what I had been."

Chapter Seven

The "Spin-Offs": Fiction and Other Prose

Deliverance (1970)

James Dickey's prose, both fiction and literary criticism, has never received the notice it deserves. His novel *Deliverance* would seem to be the exception, but the high regard in which it is now held has been a fairly recent development. The first reviews with very few exceptions did not recognize *Deliverance* as a significant work of fiction but rather judged it as an interesting work inferior to his poetry. Though not an immediate critical success, it sold well. The reasons for the initial popular success as one of the best-selling novels of 1970 were obvious. The plot had the ingredients for a surefire success, the old adventure story of hunter and hunted in a modern setting, with urban men forced to regain primitive instincts in order to kill and to survive.

Four financially successful suburbanites—Ed Gentry, Lewis Medlock, Drew Ballinger, and Bobby Trippe—plan a canoe trip down white water through wild forest country in North Georgia. Lewis is the catalyst for the others—dynamic, impressive physically, and a believer that a conditioned body is essential for survival when the machines fail. Ed Gentry provides the first-person point of view necessary for this novel. He is a partner in an Atlanta advertising agency and the director of the graphic-art department, living a life of financial adequacy but of little consequence. Drew Ballinger is a sales supervisor for a soft-drink distributor, the most content and the best adjusted of the four. Bobby Trippe sells mutual funds for a broker. He is very good at insurance but very incompetent in the woods: of the four he is physically and spiritually the weakest.

The men travel by automobile to Oree, a small backwoods town in North Georgia. Lewis and Ed persuade the redneck Grover brothers to drive their car to a pick-up point at another hamlet, Aintry. The men journey down the river and make camp. Ed begins to feel at home in the wilderness. He touches the exposed talon of an owl hunting from the roof of his tent but misses an easy bow and arrow shot at a deer visible in the fog.

The next day, back on the river, Bobby and Ed in the first canoe pull ashore to rest briefly. They are confronted by two sardonically threatening backwoodsmen, who launch a kind of taunting homosexual attack on the effeminate Bobby. Ed and Bobby are rescued by Lewis, who shoots an arrow into the chest of the older mountaineer. The younger man escapes and remains a threat to the party. Lewis persuades his accomplices to accept the death as justified and to bury the dead man.

The four continue their trip; but when they reach the worst rapids on the river, Drew collapses as if shot, capsizing the lead canoe. In the struggle through the rapids to the shore, Lewis Medlock's leg is horribly broken. Ed believes that Drew has been shot by the surviving mountaineer and that he must deliver himself and his remaining companions from this threat. A second time, a civilized man in the wilderness must kill to survive. Ed accomplishes near-miraculous feats. He climbs a sheer cliff, two hundred feet high, conceals himself in a tree, and awaits the arrival of the ambusher. When he arrives, Ed releases the arrow and mortally wounds his adversary. He accidentally injures himself by falling from the tree on one of his arrows but manages, after a torturous descent down the wall of the cliff, to commit a second body to the wilderness.

The three survivors reach Aintry, finding and concealing Drew's body on their way there. They decide to cover up everything, do not mention the mountain men, and describe Drew's death as an accident. They are questioned by the sheriff and one of his deputies and released to return to the city, changed by their experiences.

With his reviewers Dickey was less successful than with his readers. As a novelist he seemed relegated to the role of a major poet who had produced an apprentice work in fiction with all the flaws expected of a maiden voyage into another genre. He may even have been partly responsible himself for the underestimation, since Dickey has always made it clear about any prose that he wrote that his mission as a writer was as a poet. He began writing the manuscript at Positana, Italy, in 1962, and worked on it until 1969 only when he had time left over from writing the poems that appeared in *Poems 1957–1967* and in *The Eye-Beaters*.

Even though the first critical reviews were mixed, the novel stayed on the best-seller list for several months. Though not a critical success *Deliverance* had found an audience. In contrast, *The Eye-Beaters, Blood,*

Victory, Madness, Buckhead and Mercy, his first volume of poetry in three
years, and his brief account of his life as poet, *Self-Interviews,* received less
critical attention and less audience than his previous volumes of poetry and
criticism. Perhaps reacting somewhat defensively, Dickey is reported to
have said: "The *Eye-Beaters* is worth a hundred *Deliverances.*"[1]

Several of the negative reviews of *Deliverance* regarded it as primarily a
sensationalist adventure story with little or no relationship to the contemporary world. This was the same indictment that was being made against
his poetry by some critics after Robert Bly's attack on Dickey's supposed
lack of social and political consciousness.[2] Most likely reflecting the
attacks that Bly had made on Dickey, one reviewer of *Deliverance* charged:
"The world that lies outside might as well not exist for all the notice that is
taken of it."[3] Other reviewers raised complaints that were also being made
against the poetry. At a time when many writers were protesting the war
in Vietnam James Dickey, according to this view, had written a novel
glorifying violence, exploiting sexual perversion. If the novel had any
pretense to thematic significance, it was simply an expression of a kind of
mindless romanticism, what Benjamin DeMott in an influential review
described as a product of "the more life school," which he defined as
"grasping vaguely for some kind of greater absolute experience and
rejecting ordinary and normal experience."[4] There was little serious
attempt to relate themes in *Deliverance* to recurring themes in Dickey's
poetry or the plot to Dickey's long-standing interest in the importance of
narrative in poetry. This is surprising because his novel clearly bore a close
relationship to poems like "The Owl King," "Fog Envelops the Animals,"
"The Vegetable King," but most of all to the long poem "On the
Coosawattee."

Dickey has indicated that his original version of the novel was quite
different from what he published—more introverted like his poetry, more
in the style of James Agee. During the last year before the completion of
Deliverance he did a great deal of revising, stressing a straightforward novel
more and the poetic aspects of a lyrical novel less, but elements of the
original remained.[5]

The "cold war" rhetoric of Lewis Medlock about the importance of
being prepared to survive a holocaust owes something to *Deliverance*'s
origins in the political and literary contexts of the early 1960s. Movies and
television dramas then focused on the problem of survival in the aftermath
of a nuclear war. In October of 1962 fiction nearly became reality during
the Cuban missile crisis as the world waited to see if the Russians would
withdraw their long-range missiles. At this time, in Italy, Dickey began

drawing on memories of his escapes from the urban life of Atlanta to the Georgia wilderness with his friends, Lewis King, the model for Lewis Medlock, and Al Braselton.[6]

In explaining the popular appeal of *Deliverance* Dickey seems to realize that he wrote a book that deals with deliverance from both the extreme situation of survival and the ordinary situation of ennui in the modern wasteland, the city. "I wrote the right book at the right time. . . . People were caught up in a savage fable of decent men fighting for their lives and killing and getting away with it."[7]

The right time Dickey refers to was a time of anguish that Americans were suffering over the Vietnam War, culminating in the spring of 1970 in horror at the massacre at Kent State. What violence did to men and to American values was a burning issue of the times. Dickey described his intentions in choosing a subject of civilized men killing under primitive conditions: "I wrote *Deliverance* as a story where under the conditions of extreme violence people could find out things about themselves that they have no other means. . . . *Deliverance* is something that could happen."[8]

The subject may explain in part the popular success of *Deliverance*. But its critical acceptance came several years after its publication when critics began to recognize that *Deliverance* was a significant contemporary variation on one of the archetypes of American romance, the wilderness tale, perhaps a modern "anti-hero" version of the story of the great American hunter. It was also recognized as an initiation story with the added significance of being both a journey into the wilderness and down a river with suggestions of Twain's *Huckleberry Finn,* Cooper's *The Deerslayer,* and even Conrad's *Heart of Darkness.* It is rather surprising just how much archetypal significance critics have recently found in Dickey's variations on these basic plots of romance. Dickey had always indicated his interest in "big forms" in his poetry, and critics have found them in *Deliverance*—biblical references, myths, Jungian archetypes. Even a mystery was discovered: Did Ed Gentry kill the right man or did he unintentionally murder a complete stranger?[9] What previously had been regarded simply as a sensational adventure story had suddenly been found to be surprisingly complex after all.

If by the mid-1970s critics were finding unexpected significance in *Deliverance,* the novel was also gaining a cultish following among a small number of cliff-climbing enthusiasts and an enormously larger number of white-water adventurers. By the end of the 1970s Dickey had become alarmed by the number of drownings on the Chattooga River, which had served as the model for the river in the novel. Dickey's fictional river was destroyed by damming a wild river in the name of progress. Because of the popularity of the novel and of the movie, the Chattooga is threatened by an increasing number of boaters, estimated by rangers at more than 40,000 in the summer of 1980, and by a large band of professional rafters who take tourists down the river.

All of this is in part a tribute to the appeal of the beliefs of Lewis Medlock, the advocate of testing oneself in the wilderness. Lewis is the macho man of the 1970s who believes that he can set an example for others. He believes that the machines will fail and survival will depend on the readiness of the individual. "I think the machines are going to fail, the political systems are going to fail, and a few men are going to take to the hills and start over" (D, 42). Lewis still talks language appropriate for survival in the aftermath of a nuclear holocaust, but in Dickey's finished manuscript Lewis has also become the physical-fitness fanatic of the 1960s and 1970s. In his talks with Ed Gentry on this subject Lewis asserts: "I decided that survival was not in the rivets and the metal, and not in the double-sealed doors and not in the marbles or Chinese checkers. It was in me. It came down to the man, and what he could do. The body is one thing you can't fake; it's just got to be there" (D, 42).

Lewis's protégé and the novel's protagonist, Ed Gentry, has no dreams of heroic survival. He is simply a latter-day wasteland character, trapped in an urban-business, suburban-home setting typical of the late 1960s—a man who has taken the easy way through life, and as a result suffers from a sense of the inconsequence of whatever he does. Before leaving for the woods Ed describes his life to his friend Lewis as "sliding."

"I am mainly interested in sliding. Do you know what sliding is?"
"No. You want me to guess?"
"I'll tell you. Sliding is living antifriction. Or, no, sliding is living *by* antifriction. It is finding a modest thing you can do, and then greasing that thing. On both sides. It is grooving with comfort." (D, 41)

In short, Ed takes to the woods not to escape the extreme situation of a nuclear holocaust but something more everyday and ordinary, the boredom of an urban job and suburban living. The title of the novel appropriately promises not just survival but "deliverance." Since Lewis does not like his own urban business life and is so bored with ordinary life that he desires the challenge of extreme situations, he believes that his theories about conditioning have something to offer to Ed Gentry, trapped in his own life. He tells Ed: "Life is so fucked-up now, and so complicated, that I wouldn't mind if it came down, right quick, to the bare survival of who was ready to survive" (*D,* 43).

Before his journey to the wild river in northeastern Georgia the only promises for Ed Gentry of deliverance from his affluent urban wasteland have been sexual, especially the effect on him of a "gold-glowing mote" spotted in the left eye of a young model. His life has been so inconsequential that in archetypal wasteland fashion he has forgotten to notice the change of seasons and to recognize that autumn is close at hand. He is just beginning to understand his discontent. Part of his understanding comes from a vision of the monotonous sameness of the life of the secretaries. Dickey's secretaries are reminiscent of Randall Jarrell's Washington women in his poem "The Women at the Washington Zoo."[10] "The women were almost all secretaries and file clerks, young and semiyoung and middle-aged, and their hair styles, piled and shellacked and swirled and horned, and almost every one stiff, filled me with desolation" (*D,* 15).

Ed also realizes that he is not like Lewis Medlock, who "had everything that life could give, and he couldn't make it work" (*D,* 9). His discontent, he is beginning to realize, is similar to that of the artist George Holley, who had wanted to apply some of the techniques of a great artist, Georges Braque, to their advertising layouts. At the time Holley left their layout studio, Ed had been glad to see him go because then he had no wish "to surpass our limitations, or to provide a home for geniuses on their way to the Whitney or suicide" (*D,* 14). Now Ed's discontent, the change of the seasons, the thrill occasioned by the sight of the gold mote in the model's eye, and the survival rhetoric of Lewis Medlock have stirred in him the promise of "another life, deliverance" (*D,* 28). He has a shock of recognition of how the artistic sensibility of George Holley had made him as an artist feel different in the business world. George's attitude was: "I am with you but not of you" (*D,* 15).

Ed is responsive to Lewis's promise of deliverance through some kind of confrontation in the wilderness because he is becoming aware of the possibility of physical decay, that "aging with me was going to come on fast" (*D,* 29). Still Lewis's promise leaves Ed with his own Prufrockian overwhelming question: "Save Me?" I asked Lewis: "Save me from what? or for what?" (*D,* 15). The answer to that question comes only through variations on a Wordsworthian "ministry of fear and joy" in the wilderness which restores his primitive instincts and his imaginative powers. Before the journey he lacked the imagination even to ask a question about purpose.

Lewis, as Ed has suspected, will get himself and the others into an unexpected situation; for he is a hero who is accident prone, a guide who can lead others into the wilderness but not out. Dickey seems to suggest that only the man of imagination, of artistic sensibility, can do this with full understanding of what he has done.

In the wilderness the conflict becomes twofold, with nature and with man. It pits the suburbanites against the beautiful yet dangerous river. The river is, first of all, a naturalistic symbol of the indifference of nature to man. Ed Gentry is struck by this characteristic soon after their entrance into the wilderness. "It was beginning to be very wild and quiet. I remembered to be frightened and right away I was. It was the beautiful impersonality of the place that struck me the hardest; I would not have believed that it could hit me all at once like this, or with such force" (D, 80–81). The river is also a means for the journey into Dickey's own version of the heart of darkness since a much greater threat than any from the river comes from the perverted nature of the two mountain men who accost Ed and Bobby.

Some reviewers concluded somewhat hastily that Dickey had not adequately distinguished among his quartet of characters, and they even equated Ed Gentry, the protagonist, with Dickey himself. It would be more accurate to contend that Dickey once more looked within himself and found not one poetic persona but four characters who represent potential aspects of himself. Lewis Medlock is a projection of that virile Dickey, who once said that he would not object if his poetry should start a new cult of virility.[11] Lewis shares Dickey's enthusiasm for woodmanship and his archery, just as Drew Ballinger reflects Dickey, the guitarist, the admirer of folk rhythms and tunes.

Bobby Trippe in some degree caricatures Dickey the urban man, who has occasionally, in uncharacteristic moods, admitted his own inadequacies in the woods. Ed Gentry, the narrator, is Dickey in his life role as advertising man, who like the persona in *Eye-Beaters* fears middle age and seeks deliverance from routine life. Dickey certainly did not intend for Ed Gentry to be, as several reviewers believed, Lewis Medlock's apprentice. Lewis is a recognizable type in American fiction; he is the manly man who seeks a world elsewhere but cannot make a go of it. Ed fantasizes that Lewis swimming is Tarzan, who, when deprived of his heritage, regains man's primitive powers and masters the jungle. He tells Lewis before their departure from the wilderness: "What you have got is a fantasy life," to which Lewis replies: "That is all anybody has got. It depends on how strong your fantasy is, and whether you really—*really*—in your mind, fit into your own fantasy, whether you measure up to what you've fantasized. I don't know what your fantasy is, but I'll bet you don't come up to it" (*D,* 49). Lewis may not live up to his own fantasy, but he does have both a restlessness and a confidence in his own views that permit him to serve as a catalyst for Ed Gentry, who might otherwise have settled for sliding through his life in spite of his growing feeling of inconsequence. As they enter the river, Ed recognizes that Lewis

was getting me out of the rut for a while, or as he put it, "breaking the pattern."
   "Here we go," he said, out of the sleep of the mild people into the wild, rippling water." (*D,* 36)

   In many of Dickey's most important poems the persona seeks connections with "unthinking nature" during which a temporary exchange of identity occurs. In the poem "A Dog Sleeping on My Feet" the speaker imaginatively identifies briefly with the dog dreaming of a fox hunt. In "Springer Mountain" the hunter identifies with the hunted deer. In "Drinking from a Helmet" Dickey briefly exchanges identities with a dead soldier. In the process of gaining his "deliverance" from ordinary life Ed Gentry also becomes the man of imaginative sensibility capable of empathetic exchange. When the claw of the owl pierces Ed's tent, he feels himself flying with the owl. When Ed Gentry finds himself in the fog apparently disappearing into nature, he reacts as the persona does in the poem "Fog Envelops the Animals": "I feel my own long-hidden, / Long-sought invisibility / Come forth from my solid body" (*P,* 62). In *Deliverance* a deer appears to the practically invisible Ed. Perhaps because he is too conscious of how Lewis would have done it, Ed hesitates, shoots, and misses. But an even more important reason for missing is that Ed has identified with the deer empathetically. What Ed Gentry, as much more imaginative than Lewis Medlock, feels that Lewis does not is an exciting ambivalence about what he finds in nature, both terror and joy, love and brutality—a fear but at the same time a strong desire to identify with and even to surrender to unthinking nature. Ed Gentry's situation is a more extreme example of that of the speaker in Robert Frost's well-known poem "Stopping by Woods on a Snowy Evening." Both speakers feel the beauty and the threat in nature. Frost's persona rejects the pull of nature for the pull of humanity: he has promises to keep. So does Ed Gentry more reluctantly, but the effect of his experiences remains with him. While in the wilderness, he feels a oneness with nature and temporarily achieves what the great Romantic poets desired, an end to the sense of alienation between human subject and natural object. When the party takes to the river again after Lewis kills the first of the two mountain men, and Drew is (apparently) shot, Ed again feels the strong pull of the river: "I felt myself fading out into the unbelievable violence and brutality of the river, joining it. This is not such a bad way to go, I thought; maybe I am already there" (D, 144). Later, when Ed must take part in the game of hunter and hunted with the second of the two and climb the cliff to set up his ambush, he experiences a rich and complex range of feelings. "My heart expanded with joy at the thought of where I was and what I was doing. There was a new light on the water. The moon was going up and up and I stood watching the stream with my back to the rock for a few minutes not thinking of anything with a deep feeling of nakedness, helplessness, and intimacy." (D, 161).

As Ed climbs, his strength increases: "I had both hands in the cliff to the palms, and strength from the stone flowed into me" (D, 165). He climbs higher and beholds the beauty of the river: "What a view, I said again. The river was blank and mindless with beauty. It was the most glorious thing I have ever seen. But it was not seeing, really. For once it was not just seeing. It was beholding. I *beheld* the river . . ." (D, 171). What is happening is more than observation; it is participation. Ed begins to feel a part of his setting, and with a mixture of joy and fear, imagines the huge rock as something like his face. He declares: "I felt better; I felt wonderful, and fear was at the center of the feeling: fear and anticipation—there was no telling where it would end." (D, 171–72). He recalls Drew Ballinger's idea that the greatest guitarists "had developed the sense of touch beyond what a man with eyes could do" and believes that he too has recaptured a primitive sense of things: "I have got something like that, I said. I have done what I have done, I have got up here mostly by the sense of touch, and in the dark" (D, 172).

Ed has empathy as well as fear for the man with whom he is engaged in the deadly game of hunter and hunted. To Lewis Medlock it would have been a game and a test, but to Ed it is a primitive act about which he feels a powerful ambivalence. He is caught between the human and the natural, between feeling and indifference. Ed says, "It was the same state of mind that I had when I hunted the deer in the fog. These were worthy motions I was going through, but only motions, and it was shocking to remind myself that if I came on him with the rifle I would have to carry them through or he would kill me" (D, 175).

Ed feels the Dionysian irrational and Apollonian rational polarities within himself, the strength of a "noon blazing sexuality" and the countering pull of the human. He glories in his emotions but struggles against their dominance: "And yet I held madly to the human. I looked for a slice of gold like the model's in the river; some kind of freckle, something lovable in the huge serpent-shape of light" (D, 176).

When he shoots his prey, Ed again feels the conflicting impulses of engagement and indifference: "I had thought so long and hard about him that to this day I still believe that I felt, in the moonlight, our minds fuse. It was not that I felt myself turning evil but than an enormous physical indifference, as vast as the whole abyss of light at my feet, came to me: an indifference not only to the other man's body scrambling and kicking on the ground with an arrow through it, but also to mine" (D, 180). As he kills, and accidentally wounds himself, Ed identifies with his victim; and there is a brief moment of exchange of identity. But after the dying man's movements cease, the exchange begins to dissipate. Ed looks on the body of the man he killed and thinks: "His brain and mine unlocked and fell apart, and in a way I was sorry to see it go. I had never thought with another man's mind on life and death, and would never think that way again" (D, 199). The experience is similar to the contradictory feelings of the speaker in many of Dickey's poems, ranging from the involvement felt by the soldier in "Drinking from a Helmet," where his mind fuses momentarily with that of the dead soldier from whose helmet he has drunk and which he has donned, to the detachment of the aviator, now suburbanite, in "The Firebombing."

But the fusion is always temporary. Ed's mind and that of the man he killed unlock. He feels a strong primitive desire within himself to mutilate, perhaps even to cannibalize the body of his victim, but it passes. "It did not come, but the ultimate horror circled me and played over the knife. I began to sing. It was a current popular favorite, a folk-rock tune. I finished and I was withdrawn from" (D, 200). After he has delivered his party from death, Ed feels contempt for Bobby Trippe, who has been unmanned by the woods as well as by the two mountain men. Looking down from the heights of the cliff on Bobby in the approaching boat below, Ed draws a practice bead on the middle of Bobby's chest and caught up once more in dangerous forces he cannot completely understand, he says, "it had been close, very close" (D, 202).

Ed not only delivers himself, Lewis, and Bobby from the threats of the river and from the mountain men but finds what Dickey believes the poet should find through writing his poems—"a new or insufficiently known part of himself" (*S,* 164). He has engaged in the same process of exchange with "unthinking nature" that occurs in many of Dickey's poems. His experience is frightening as well as joyous, and his final deliverance must be from the spiritual dangers of such an exchange.

Benjamin DeMott found in *Deliverance,* as he found in Dickey's poetry, an expression of the desire of "the more life school" for "the generative power at the core of existence." According to DeMott, "A first-rate Dickey poem breathes the energy of the world and testifies the poet's capacity for rising out of trenched darkness, an habitual, half-lived life into a more intensive appetitiveness of being"[12] It would be more exact to say that Dickey as neo-romantic is concerned with the regenerative powers nature may offer to contemporary man but also that he is a post-Darwinian writer aware of the dangers inherent in the regression to primitive powers. Dickey has identified an early influence on his thinking which "has been in my mind ever since,"[13] a review of several books on mythology by Stanley Edgar Hyman in the *Kenyon Review.* Hyman cites from mythology "'a separation from the world, a penetration to some source of power and a life enhancing return.'" Dickey concludes: "If there's any literary precedent to *Deliverance,* it's that passage as I encountered it quoted by Stanley Edgar Hyman, referring to Van Gennep's concept of the *rites de passage.*"

If what Ed Gentry as artistic sensibility sees is what *Deliverance* means, then what he sees and learns is a modern version of the romantic vision of a ministry of fear and joy in nature stressing the necessity of holding on to the human and controlling some of the emotions which gave him the power to kill in order to survive. Ed Gentry finds the act of killing and empathizing with his victim so natural and even joyous an act that the possibility of killing again is a close thing.

The critical success of *Deliverance* as a novel of consequence has just recently matched the popular success of the novel as a rather shocking adventure story. Mythological and archetypal readings, even Jungian interpretations, suggest that Dickey has caught in this novel something far more than the average adventure story. He may even have pricked the American collective unconscious with a desire to return to frontier conditions. Yet the most conspicuous reference is biblical, the quotation from the book of Obadiah that precedes the text of the novel:

> The pride of thine heart hath deceived thee,
>   thou that dwellest in the clefts of the rock,
>   whose habitation is high; that saith in his heart,
>   Who shall bring me down to the ground?

It has been suggested that this epigraph is intended to apply to Lewis Medlock, who is brought low and must leave the deliverance of his party of explorers to this pupil, Ed Gentry. This is true. The Lewis Medlock at the end of the novel is humbled. He walks with a limp and Ed realizes, "He can die now; he knows that dying is better than immortality. He is a human being, and a good one" (*D,* 277). The river has happened to Lewis in that he no longer desires to be superhuman; he can no longer be seen as Ed Gentry once saw him, as Tarzan.

But it is actually Ed Gentry who dwells in the cliffs of the rock, where he feels with indifference the power of life and death over others as when he targets Bobby; and it is he who must return from his physical and emotional heights to the ground, to the normal life of the city, where he cannot live with indifference to others. The actual river is lost in the huge lake that the dam created. It remains with Ed as "a personal, private possession, as nothing else in me ever had. . . . The river underlies, in one way or another, everything I do" (*D,* 275–76).

It has led Ed to realize that he needs a second deliverance: he must return to the human. It is his wife, his family, and his friend George Holley who must now save him. Ed realizes on his return: "They were going to save me, here" (*D,* 269). "The main thing was to get back into my life and quickly and as deeply as I could; as if I had never left it" (*D,* 274). Ed may have transcended the inconsequence of his ordinary life, but he must now accept the lesser life and live on the human plane with knowledge of the difference. The other life will always mean something to him, but it belongs back with the lost river and remains only as a "private, personal possession," his own version of Wordsworth's "emotion recollected in tranquility." Ed has experienced a kind of artistic awakening; he is no longer sliding since he still feels the deliverance of the river.

The novel is well named: the subject is deliverance. Lewis Medlock is the catalyst who provides the grounds for Ed Gentry's deliverance from his life of inconsequence. Lewis delivers Bobby and Ed from the initial threat of the mountain men. Then Ed must carry on for the injured Lewis and deliver the three suburbanites from the threat of the man Lewis does not kill. He must also prevent their crime from being discovered. Finally, Ed needs deliverance from the primitive power he has discovered in nature and unleashed in himself. He recognizes this when he returns home to Martha. He renounces the primitive but gains a kind of artistic rebirth. He attempts new collages and hires back Braque enthusiast George Holley. "George has become my best friend, next to Lewis, and we do a lot of serious talking about art; more than we should, with the work load the studio has been accumulating" (*D,* 276).

In the novel Dickey has assimilated two major events of his life. He has elaborated upon his weekend and summer canoeing escapes from the business of advertising with his two Atlanta friends, Lewis King and Al Braselton. He enjoyed hinting to his agent and to his publisher that the fiction might have actually happened on one of these adventures. What actually happened was a withdrawal from a life of inconsequence in advertising without a return to it. In 1963 Dickey quit his job in advertising and risked all on barnstorming for poetry.

Other Prose

James Dickey has promised, but not finished, a second novel. He describes it in some detail in *Sorties* as *Death's Baby Machine,* a novel about flying. Somewhere in the process of slow composition the conception seemed to change, and the title definitely did, to *Alnilam.* The only segment published so far appeared in *Esquire* in 1976 under the title "Cahill is Blind."[14] The episode is based on Dickey's feelings when he was himself temporarily blinded while posing for the mask that is pictured on the cover of that issue of *Esquire.* It would suggest a shift toward a more lyric novel, for what Dickey has written here is an attempt to give stream-of-consciousness perceptions from the other five senses as a blind man attempts to perform all his vital functions, including sex. The style is close to that of Dickey's volume of poetry, *The Zodiac.*

If Dickey left the business world for poetry, he returned there in the judgment of many reviewers with the publication of *Jericho: The South Beheld* in 1974. This was an enormously successful commercial venture, published by Oxmoor Press, a subsidiary of the *Progressive Farmer,* also the publisher of *Southern Living.* The result was a luxury book, illustrated by artist Hubert Shuptrine, with prose poems by Dickey. Through courtesy of the subscription lists of *Southern Living* and *Progressive Farmer, Jericho* entered many southern homes where Dickey's poems were unknown and perhaps even unwelcome. It was a handsome volume on the landscape and people of the South suitable for display on the book shelf, or, even more appropriately, on the coffee table. The book was not necessarily something to be read through, but rather sampled, or as the title rather ironically suggests, even "beheld."

Jericho deserves praise as a different kind of a work from what Dickey or any other serious poet has attempted recently, and as a product of considerable talent for advertising (as critics were quick to point out), as well as a creative achievement. Dickey had seemingly turned from what he had always proclaimed his mission as a literary artist, poetry, to a prose work intended for a popular audience and from publication by a major commercial publisher to a small (as far as book publication is concerned), private publisher interested in luxury editions. It is hard to imagine a reader of *Jericho: The South Beheld* or of Dickey's next venture in this genre, *God's Images,* as an appreciative reader of important, sometimes controversial, Dickey poems like "Slave Quarters" or "The Sleep Child." Dickey's success could be regarded as evidence of his versatility, of his ability to "make connections" with different kinds of readers.

Both *Jericho* and *God's Images* are useful works for anyone who believes that Dickey's works are of a piece, since there are in these works some of the same themes recurring in his poetry, in his fiction, and in his literary criticism. It is as if, not able at this time to make substantial creative use of these themes in poetry, or to complete his second novel, *Alnilam,* he had decided to test his skill at taking some of his old themes and a new subject to a different and new audience.

Jericho is an acknowledgment of Dickey's southern heritage, or of his poet's eye for southern landscape, and of even an Agrarian love of the land. The major change, or perhaps concession, to his new audience is that Dickey no longer appears in his role of poet of the expansive imagination compelling belief in creative lies in which he transcends the literal self and commonplace situations.

Writing about the South, present and past, for an audience he knows from his southern-based advertising stints, Dickey drew on the shared heritage of southern writer and reader. Dickey comments in his introduction: "This is no book about the magnolia-and-moonlight South, though come to think of it, a magnolia tree seen through binoculars—or even without them—is as crazily significant and as beautiful as anything on earth. No, it is an attempt to get down through the sense of sight and words what Hubert and I have lived, and to present it to the rest of you" (*J,* 17).

In *Jericho,* Dickey seems to have shifted the burden of imagination from the writer who imagines for the reader to the reader who must imagine for himself and become a "Beholder." A "beholder" is one who "enters into objects and people and places with the sense of these things entering into him" (*J,* 15). Dickey also makes it clear what he wants his beholders to do: to go "deeply into human life . . . of our particular segment of the world and what it offers . . . to those familiar with it by birth . . . and those who come to the South as strangers . . ." (*J,* 17).

The perspective in *Jericho* is from the flight of a sea gull (Dickey's favorite form for reincarnation) who journeys with the reader across southern landscape from St. Augustine, the South's oldest city, to Birmingham, a symbol of the industrialized new South. The southern landscape, seen from the eye of the gull, is both natural and man-made. This dual nature of the landscape signifies the two movements that have motivated southerners in utilization of the land—the older Agrarian tradition and the new South industrialization. The South that Dickey wants beheld as Jericho, as the Promised Land as well as the city whose walls fell, is based on a precarious and fragile fusion of these two forces, what nature has given and what man has wrought.

Jericho is a work of parts, not a satisfactory whole. There are some good images and vivid scenes, which, appropriately for his sea-gull beholder, Dickey calls "flickers." If we do not have the usual Dickey persona or a surrogate, the poem still manages a sense of things being said—always a Dickey strength. What is surprising from a poet who has been critical of academicism in poetry is the number of literary allusions in the book, echoes of Dickey's own poems and themes, and of other southern poets—John Crowe Ransom, Allen Tate, and Donald Davidson. These allusions are appropriately southern for a southern book.

God's Images is less successful, and even more academic, with Dickey ambitiously challenging Blake, Milton, and the translators of the King James Bible. It is a less successful book because it lacks even what unity *Jericho* has and the conversational vigor of that book which comes from a consistent narrative voice. *God's Images* attempts to present many different voices. Though Dickey does not explicitly acknowledge it, he is engaged in *God's Images,* and in the volume of poetry that followed it, *The Zodiac,* in what Robert Lowell and other poets have called "imitations," recasting the images and rhythms of other poets in his own idiom.

There seems to be no overall thesis, certainly no intention as grandiose as a Miltonic "justifying the ways of God to man." Dickey is engaged in trying to actualize as a poet the images from the Bible "buried and alive in us all" (*GI,* 3). He hopes to expose the unconscious heritage of his reader. What is more certain is his success in providing suitable verbal images and brief explications of the visual texts created by Marvin Hayes's etchings.

Many reviewers regarded *Jericho: The South Beheld* and *God's Images* as strictly commercial ventures. Dickey intended a bit more. He wanted to establish connections between poet and artist and readers with a shared southern Protestant heritage. The two artists in different media draw images from their own "inner kingdoms." This intention is stated in *God's*

Images; the execution is better realized in *Jericho: The South Beheld.* Yet the desire is an authentic one. Dickey's interest in coffee-table books has now turned to the setting of his novel *Deliverance,* Appalachia, for a word-and-picture study, once more with painter Hubert Shuptrine, of the land and people of that diminishing region, tentatively titled *Wilderness of Heaven.*[15]

Chapter Eight

The Literary Criticism, Lately Neglected

The "Suspect" in Poetry

James Dickey's career as a literary critic began when he was poetry editor and reviewer for the *Sewanee Review*. There he developed something of a reputation as a "hatchet man" who deftly chopped down the reputations of poets he did not respect. Robert Penn Warren, later a friend and admirer, recalls: "When James Dickey came to my attention as a reviewer, I thought he was one of the roughest around."[1] This reputation was not quite deserved since Dickey's critical hatchet was reserved only for what he called in the first collection of his reviews the "suspect" in poetry. Dickey's reviews were perceived variously as entertaining, opinionated, sometimes harsh, displaying an excess of ego; but not, as they might well be regarded in retrospect, as important contributions to Dickey's own vision of a freer, personal, but still carefully crafted postmodernist poetry. Style and tone were admired more than substance.

There are other reasons for James Dickey's meager reputation as a literary critic. First of all, he began as a poetry reviewer, and he has continued to express his critical ideas outside formal critical performances—writing not essays but additional reviews, giving numerous interviews, and tape recording for publication one uniquely egocentric volume—*Self-Interviews*. Second, the personality of Dickey, his "unrepressed ego," was always much in evidence in what he wrote, to the annoyance of some of his reviewers; the consequence of Dickey's intense subjectivity has been to obscure the importance of his contributions as poet-critic as well as the relationship of intensely held critical ideas to his poetry. Finally, Dickey has also contributed to the critical disregard for his literary criticism through his own statements about what he has done. He has, for example, disavowed his first major collection of his reviews, *Babel to Byzantium*, as a "full-scale critical performance," modestly asserting that he knows "any reasonably good student of aesthetics could tear [my] 'ideas' apart with no trouble."[2] This pose of a dabbler has been held consistently in regard to his prose; Dickey's position has always been that his "preoccupation is with poetry, and everything else is a spin-off from that—novels, literary criticism, screen plays, whatever."[3]

The reviews reprinted from the *Sewanee Review* in *The Suspect in Poetry* and in *Babel to Byzantium* are much less polemic than their reputation would suggest. When told of Robert Penn Warren's impression of his roughness on poets in his early days as a poetry reviewer, Dickey demurred: "Well, I'm not all that rough. I have a very naive feeling as a reviewer. I don't believe that a reviewer or a critic can really criticize well unless he can praise well. I always liked that about Randall Jarrell. He praised well. James Agee praises well. You've got to be able to like the right things to be enabled to dislike the wrong things."[4] What Dickey's statement about Jarrell ignores is that Jarrell's reputation in his early days as a reviewer was much the same as Dickey's own for roughness. Dickey's harsh reputation may have resulted from his ability to express his negative judgments wittily and memorably: "[J. V.] Cunningham is a good, deliberately small and authentic poet, a man with tight lips, a good education, and his own agonies. His handsome little book should be read, and above all by future Traditionalists and Compressors; he is their man." (*BB*, 194).

Dickey is clearly not "their man" and he makes that abundantly clear. What he does like and praises well is less memorable, and his reasons are clear only when what he wrote then is read along with the essays in his later volume, *Sorties*. What he does not like in his early criticism is any kind of academicism, especially "the university-taught" garden variety poets or "the School of Charm" (*BB*, 10).

In his earliest *Sewanee Review* criticism Dickey stresses that the first step in restoring meaning to poetry is by compelling the reader's belief through establishing "the presence of a living being," creating "a distinctive poetic voice" (*BB*, 107). Two other requirements are made of the poets he reviews. The poet must also earn belief, establish a connection between poet and reader, by making "effective *statements,* ones you believe, and believe in, at first sight . . ." (*BB*, 151). Dickey also prefers "a basis of narrative," through describing or depicting "an action" in poetry, and regaining for poetry what it had lost to fiction (*BB*, 287).

Babel to Byzantium: Vision and Form

The essays in *The Suspect in Poetry* and in *Babel to Byzantium* were written during the late 1950s and the early 1960s at a time when Randall Jarrell and Karl Shapiro were also in their different ways breaking with "new critical" formalism and the modernist tradition that had favored impersonality, mythology, and academicism in poetry. Dickey was in his own way nurturing the same seeds of change as Jarrell and Shapiro. Among the older generation of poets, William Carlos Williams, who had long had his differences with the Eliot brand of modernism, was an influence on the new directions being taken by Allen Ginsberg and Robert Lowell in the 1950s. Dickey also admired Williams at his best, but his view of Williams's poetry was somewhat different from theirs. Williams's best poems demonstrate how one can be close to the surfaces of life while avoiding the commonplace. The commonplace is clearly as foreign to Dickey's concept of good poetry as the university-oriented academicism of many modernist poets. Williams is better than his imitators because he transcends the commonplace by instant symbolization: his poetry has its magic "moments when a commonplace event or object is transfigured without warning . . ." (*BB*, 244).

Dickey not only demands that good poems of other poets be both nonacademic and nonliteral, but he also commends to his reader his own penchant for "'the big basic forms'—rivers, mountains, woods, clouds, oceans . . ." (*BB*, 291). For Dickey it is the commitment to both ". . . vision and to the backbreaking craft of verse" that makes the good poet. His exemplars in this respect are Roethke, Rilke, and D. H. Lawrence, who are, he declares, the "great empathizers" and "the awakeners," who can go beyond the commonplace and even "change your life" by compelling belief in what they write through "inducing you to believe that you were *meant* to perceive things" as they present them" (*BB*, 149). It is when poetry accomplishes this goal that it becomes the kind of magical thing Dickey believes it should be.

When Dickey attempts to describe the kind of substance he likes in poetry, he may owe something to the New Critics' praise of "tension" in poetry. Dickey's version is a preference for a tonal complexity that comes from a "sense of being glad to be alive to write that particular poem" but also from outrage at the possibility of the loss of all things that have meant much to him—a sense of "outrage that these personal, valuable things could ever be definitely lost for anyone" (*BB*, 281). In describing the poets he admires most, Dickey identifies his kind of tension. In Theodore

Roethke the tension is the ability of Roethke to be "not far from total despair" but also "not far from total joy" (*BB*, 151); and in Edwin Arlington Robinson, the poet he admires almost equally with Roethke, it is his "desperately poised uncertainty" (*BB*, 223).

In a key essay in *Babel to Byzantium*, "The Poet Turns on Himself," Dickey's concern is consistent with the emphasis in the essays in his later books, *Self-Interviews* and *Sorties*. It is in this essay that the significance of his title *Babel to Byzantium* becomes evident; each poet has his own vision, his vision of Byzantium. To actualize this vision he is dependent on a flow of images from the memory, even out of the subconscious, but it requires the right language and the proper form. Dickey clearly regards his own best poetic efforts and those of the poets he values the most as an attempt to find the language necessary to "incarnate" those moments which are "most persistent and obsessive" in the memory (*BB*, 292). Dickey was supportive of the new freedom in the poetry of the 1950s and the 1960s, but to earn his praise a poet must also be a craftsman who can maintain a proper balance between the passion of his visions and the formal demands of language. The poet must use his talent with language to find among the many tongues of Babel the right words for his Byzantium—the vision he desires to communicate. Unfortunately, as his brief reviews make clear, in his judgment, many contemporary poets fail at the one extreme or the other, producing either vision without the necessary craftsmanship or the craftsmanship without the vision. His reviews specify the failures.

Self-Interviews

The most representative essay in *Babel to Byzantium*, revealing Dickey as almost as much the subject of his essays as the poet he is reviewing, is Dickey's essay on Randall Jarrell. Dickey conducts a dialogue with himself as critic, who responds intellectually and judgmentally to Jarrell's poetry, and as a poet, who responds emotionally and empathetically to Jarrell's successes and failures as a fellow poet.

A reviewer who had taken careful note of Dickey's Jarrell dialogue would have been less surprised by Dickey's next book of criticism, *Self-Interviews* (1970), than most of his reviewers were. This book of tape talk was the product of Dickey's response via tape recorder to questions about himself and his poetry asked by coeditors James and Barbara Reiss. The volume is slender, but seldom has a contemporary poet told more about himself as author than Dickey has in this volume and in his next, *Sorties* (1971). The confessionalism that Dickey had denied the poet seems more acceptable to him in his own prose. The dialogue in the Jarrell essay has become monologue, the distinctive voice of James Dickey speaking on himself, occasionally at his best, but also at his worst. *Self-Interviews* is nevertheless valuable as a handbook of information on Dickey as poet and as repudiation of T. S. Eliot's formalism, both his doctrine of impersonality for modern poetry and his practice of expressing his critical ideas in carefully crafted essays that advance the art of that form. Dickey also seems bent on rejecting another formalist tenet, dear to the New Critics, the intentional fallacy, their exposure as a fallacy the belief that a writer's own statements about his works can exhaust the possible meanings of those works. To New Critics like Cleanth Brooks or Robert Penn Warren nothing except a close explication of the literary text by a critic can reveal the actual meaning as opposed to the intended meaning. *Self-Interviews* is Dickey's testimony to his belief that a poet's statements about origins and personal meanings of a work can be of value in understanding it.

Part one of *Self-Interviews,* "The Poet at Mid-Career," traces the development of Dickey's creative psyche from his earliest creative efforts to the publication of his first major collection, *Poems 1957–1967.* Part two, "The Poem as Something That Matters," is divided into five sections, one for each of his first five volumes of poetry. The coverage is extensive: practically every major poem Dickey has written is discussed. Dickey is descriptive of his intentions; but he is seldom prescriptive about meanings, since he is not trying to preclude anybody else's interpretation. His accounts of the origins of his poems are anecdotal and entertaining re-creations of the creative act, such as Allen Tate undertook in his classic essay on his poem "Ode to the Confederate Dead."

Self-Interviews is nevertheless a product of Dickey's staunch faith in his memory; it expresses his belief in the importance of drawing on and building on the best of his memories that come up from out of "that strange limbo between conscious memory and the unconscious, where remembered things have what physicists call a half-life" (*SI,* 55).

The informal autobiography of the mind of the poet that begins in *Self-Interviews* and continues in the "Journals" section of his next book, *Sorties,* is largely an account of the connections Dickey has made in his poetry and also of his convictions as poet-critic on how these connections are best made. He indicates that he has always desired to achieve "presentational immediacy" in his poetry in the belief that this quality would lead to the kind of reader involvement with poetry that good writers of prose fiction get. In his poetry the poet will be concerned with many disparate subjects, but he must present them concretely enough to communicate to his readers a convincing illusion that there is a connection among all the different strands of divergence.

Above all, Dickey stresses the importance of memory to the poet, and he unabashedly uses himself as his own exemplar. To Dickey the poet values "remembered things," and he cannot bear to believe that they will ever "be totally expunged" (*SI,* 57). He writes his poems with the intention of preserving both the memories and the passion that they occasion which permit the creation of the poem. The memories are subject to the changes that linguistic structure may necessitate, and the poet's "censor" should eliminate what might be aesthetically bad. Beyond this Dickey will not go. He is entirely opposed to T. S. Eliot's antiromantic dictum that the poet must find objective correlatives and transmute his personal emotions into impersonal artistic feelings. On the contrary, Dickey has a neoromantic faith that emotions can lead to creativity. He declares: "I want to try to conserve the passion, wind it up tight like a spring so that it always has that sense of energy and compression, that latency which is always available to anyone who looks for it" (*SI,* 65). He desires to preserve the instinctual life that is left to civilized man, and he envies in animals the "instinctual notion of how much energy to expend, the ability to do a thing thoughtlesly and do it right . . ." (*SI,* 60). Dickey is a neoromantic in his faith and in instinctual life and a post-Darwinian poet in his belief in the possibility of of regressing and regaining temporarily the instincts and extrarational powers that man has just about evolved out of. He imagines this possibility in his poetry and in his novel *Deliverance.* In *Self-Interviews* he proclaims his faith in this resource for his creative imagination: "There's a part of me that has never heard of a telephone. By an act of will I can call up the whole past which includes telephones, but there is a half-dreaming, half-animal part of me that is fundamentally primitive. I really believe this, and I try to get it into poems; I don't think this quality should die out of people" (*SI,* 68–69).

One might say that James Dickey has his own version of the dissociation of sensibility between thought and feeling that preoccupied T. S. Eliot in his concern for the modern poet. Eliot saw a split between thought and feeling; Dickey sees modern man deprived of instinctual life. If this quality does die out of people, it will be a result of the premium contemporary society places on specialization. The price of specialization is "the loss of a sense of intimacy with the natural process" (*SI,* 68). For a more unified sensibility the poet must establish connections with the great mystery of process in nature, with "the great natural cycles of birth and death, the seasons, the growing up of plants and the dying of the leaves, the generations of animals and of men . . ." (*SI,* 68). It is this kind of connection that permits good poetry, in Dickey's view, to transcend the commonplace and become magical. Modernist poetry has been predominantly concerned with man in the modern wasteland, the city. The natural world is more important to Dickey than the man-made world. His Vanderbilt predecessors lamented the passing of an agrarian way of life in the South. Dickey laments with D. H. Lawrence that "as a result of our science and industrialization, we have lost the cosmos" (*SI,* 67).

Sorties

The "Journals" section of Dickey's 1971 volume of essays, *Sorties,* is a continuation of the artistic self-analysis begun in *Self-Interviews.* There are, however, differences. The entries are in the form of scattered notes, and they are written at a time of actual engagement in creative work rather than in retrospect, as in *Self-Interviews.* The material is even more personal and intimate than in the previous volume, and as much as Dickey dislikes the term, even confessional.

Once more, Dickey deliberately avoids the formal critical performance, preferring to express his critical ideas in a more personal and intimate form than the formal critical essay permits. The form chosen is traditional, since notebooks and journals have always been an important part of a writer's creative activity even though not always intended for the public. It would not be accurate to say that Dickey does not write critical essays, for in *Sorties* he includes five essays written originally as lectures and for special occasions as well as a brief epilogue for the volume. Unfortunately, adverse critical responses to what seemed the deliberately egocentric presence of Dickey's own personality obscured for some reviewers the importance of the essays to an understanding of Dickey's intentions in his poetry and of his contributions to a postmodernist literary criticism. *Sorties* and *Self-Interviews* were seemingly just too much of a self-congratulatory ego trip through Dickey's own memories and critical prejudices to be taken seriously as literary criticism. The personality of Dickey in print had become almost as evident as in his enormously successful, though occasionally controversial, public readings. There was another reason for a definite note of hostility toward Dickey. As a southern poet who had not perceptibly participated in the protest movement against the war in Vietnam he had become suspect among liberals. The case against Dickey was presented by his former friend and the publisher of *The Suspect in Poetry,* Robert Bly.[5] According to Webster a "sortie" is "a sally of troops from a besieged place against the besiegers." Dickey had chosen the right title for another book of criticism. His new book and his reputation were both under minor siege. The quantity of Dickey's production of poetry, and in the view of some reviewers, the quality, too, had declined. Dickey was apparently giving too much of himself and writing too little of literary consequence. A judgment of contemporary criticism of poetry offered near the beginning of *Sorties* might be applied to his own work: "Contemporary criticism of poetry: far too much is made of far too little. The critic is attempting to be more ingenious and talented than the poem, and stands on his head to be original: that is, to *invent* an originality for the poems that can come to them only through him" (*S,* 6).

The personal equation in *Sorties* is intentional, and it is of value for what it reveals about the relationship between Dickey and the critical personae that he has created. All the Dickey self-stances appear. There is the macho Dickey, who said that, if he is not an advocate of virility in contemporary literature, he would not object if assigned that role.[6] He occasionally sounds like his own fictional creation, Lewis Medlock: "The body is the one thing you cannot fake. It is what it is, and it does what it does. It also fails to do what it cannot do. It would seem to me that people would realize this, especially men" (*S,* 4). He also appears as a Whitmanesque, intensified man as poet who would change his reader and even a good bit of his world:

What I want to do most as a poet is to charge the world with vitality: with the vitality that it already has, if we could rise to it. This vitality can be expressed in the smallest thing and in the largest; from the ant heaving at a grain of sand to the stars straining not to be extinguished. (*S,* 5)

Whitman could not have asked for much more.

In striking contrast, Dickey also gives his reader a brief glimpse of a self he usually tries to conceal, that of the university professor who as a poet avoids writing academic poetry but who enjoys the professorial life. He confesses: "It is a marvelous thing, this having a house full of books. Something crosses the mind—a flash of light, some connection, some recognition—and one simply rises from one's chair and goes, as though by predestination, to that book, to that poem" (*S,* 5–6).

More often Dickey appears as one of the "roughs," as a poet who prefers the open life and open forms in literature to the urban or academic life and to the closed forms preferred by modernists and formalists. He does not "like the locked-in quality of formalist verse." Formalists desire the impression of coming "at an effect of inevitability. There are lots of other kinds of inevitability than this, and the best of these do not have the sense of claustrophobia that formalist verse has" (*S*, 8–9). Formalists prefer compression. Dickey makes his preference clear. "I want, mainly, the kind of poetry that opens out, instead of closes down" (*S*, 9).

Dickey may prefer open forms, and he admires "power" and a sense of "abandon" in poetry; but he never advocates uncontrolled or critically uncensored spontaneity. The neoromantic in Dickey may advocate openness and freedom; but the formalist, the worker with language, counters with the case for artistic control and careful craftsmanship. He tells himself to play with "confidence, power, and relaxation" and to add "abandon." But then he adds as equally important: "To that, add precision" (*S*, 9). He urges himself to revise—to get it right: "*Phrase* it, *phrase* it. One cannot work too much on such a thing" (*S*, 10).

In still another Whitmanesque stance Dickey extols his own poetic sensibility, assuring himself that he has a greater "accessibility to experience" than even Henry James ever had and affirming his memory for those things which mean something to him. He offers himself as an example of what in the personality of a writer makes him a writer. He is his own representative poet, "born with some kind of extra sensitivity to things" and capacity "to receive impressions" and to retain them because "they *mean* something to him." Things "matter" to him; he feels for them and remembers them (*S*, 20–21).

Not all is egotism or egocentric. Dickey is aware of writing, after a period of critical formalism, on the personality of the poet in relation to his works in a great romantic tradition, part Wordsworthian self-analysis of the mind of the poet and part Whitmanesque assertion of the importance of the self in a poetry in which a celebration of life is still possible.

Part II of *Sorties* consists of Dickey's largest collection of critical essays so far, six in all, and a brief epilogue. Two essays were talks given while Dickey was poetry consultant at the Library of Congress—"Metaphor as Pure Adventure" and "Spinning the Crystal Ball." Two are reprints of reviews of biographies, of Louis Coxe's biography of Edwin Arlington Robinson,[9] and of Allen Seager's biography of Theodore Roethke.[8] These reviews are as much concerned with the poet as with poetry. The remaining two essays, "The Self as Agent" and "The Son, the Cave, and the Burning Bush," were originally included in anthologies.[9] In all of these essays the approach is personal and subjective, with little or no objective explication of poetic texts. The reader is given instead Dickey's opinions, which come more from his interests as a poet than from his role as a literary critic. Dickey is obviously expanding on ideas and judgments he has made in his previous interviews and reviews. The difference in *Sorties* is his concern for the lives, the individual existential situations, of the poets he considers compared to their goals and accomplishments, a subject that had much personal meaning for Dickey himself in the 1970s as his poetic output began to slow down. He is struck by the contradictions between the affirmative in the poems and the destructiveness in the lives of the poets.

The final essay in *Sorties* is one of Dickey's best. "The Self as Agent" is a significant essay on a subject of great importance to Dickey as an opponent of impersonality in poetry—the role of the self in the poem. The view here is not exactly unbridled romanticism. Dickey's romantic tendencies are once more moderated by his Vanderbilt New Critical heritage. Form is important, as is content. The "I" in the poem is more than the ordinary self. The poet's obligation is not just to tell the literal truth but rather to "make" his truth so that "the vision of the poem will impose itself on the reader as more memorable and value-laden than the actuality it is taken from" (*S*, 156). The theme of participation in the poem by both poet and reader is restated. His emphasis here is on what the poem does for the poet more than for the reader. A good poem is also a participation in a self-discovery. "During the writing of the poem the poet comes to feel that he is releasing into its proper field of response a portion of himself he has never really understood" (*S*, 157). The self is essential in the poem because it is the agent that helps the poet to "discover" his poem. Dickey's preference is for the I-poem and the I-narration because the poet in Dickey's view "is capable of inventing or bringing to light out of himself a very large number of I-figures to serve in different poems . . ." (*S*, 161). For the poet "the chief glory and excitement of writing poetry" comes from this "chance to confront and dramatize parts of himself that otherwise would not have surfaced" (*S*, 161). The poet is providing for his reader, through participating in a self-discovery, a sensation of emotional truth. Poetry is a kind of experiential knowledge: the poet "has a new or insufficiently known part of himself released," and he is able to convey this knowledge convincingly to the reader as humanly important emotional truth (*S*, 161). If Dickey does not quite provide the rationale for such theories, appropriately for a critic who values personality, he does reiterate his personal beliefs with the conviction that comes from the experience of his own practice.

Dickey's literary criticism is a criticism of fragments—short reviews, brief introductions, public lectures, interviews, self-interviews tape recorded. He has expressed consistent attitudes, though he has not attempted to organize his critical essays as clearly around a theme, as Allen Tate, Karl Shapiro, and Randall Jarrell have done with a greater consistency. He does not rank poets though he gives candid judgments of individual poets; nor is Dickey the spokesman for any kind of great tradition in modern poetry as his Vanderbilt predecessors Tate, Brooks, and Warren were. A comparison with Randall Jarrell is apt because Dickey admired Jarrell and because, like Dickey, Jarrell broke with formalist theory and practice, restored the poet to the poem and the personality of the critic to literary criticism. Jarrell, in *Poetry and the Age,* and Dickey, consistently in his criticism, desire the readers to be participants in the poems they read.

Dickey's criticism is pertinent to postmodernism in poetry and to postformalism in criticism. His approach to criticism is subjective, not objective and hermeneutical, and his view of the poem is as a dramatization of unrealized aspects of the ego of the poet rather than as a self-contained or autotelic artifact. Dickey has been a determined spokesman for connections between the author and his poem without deteriorating into a poetry of literalism or of commonplaces. He seeks significant connections between persona of the poem and the reader that can compel belief in a transcendence of the ordinary limitations of the self. He is aware of the destructive forces in nature, but he regards himself as a poet like Theodore Roethke, as a celebrator of life. If Dickey is a believer in possibilities of meaning in art and in life, he is also aware of the dangers of a complete surrender to the instincts and to the emotions—of becoming like "unthinking nature." If he is neoromantic in his preference for open forms and in his penchant for personality, he is also an advocate of balance between the demands of form and the freedom required for inspiration. In short, Dickey is for Dionysian passion but also for Apollonian control.

James Dickey's favorite myth seems to be that of Orpheus. He has used it in his poetry and in his novel *Deliverance.* There is also a kind of orphic stance in his literary criticism. He has a strong sense of the mission of the poet as the one with the power to make things happen in the imagination of his readers. Yet his poet, and he is his own chief example, is a grateful survivor of chaos who can still be a celebrant of life in spite of the inevitable "dismemberments" of men, not by Thracian women but by war, age, and disease.

Dickey's poems of the 1970s, though few in number, suggest a change to more objective personae who are not Dickey himself but others who serve as surrogates. Because he has written very few critical essays in the 1970s, there is no comparable discernible shift from his consistent advocacy of the subjective in poetry to championing anything like "objective correlatives" for personal feelings, although the critical essays he has written recently are less personal, less controversial, and less significant than the earlier ones.

In 1979 Dickey gave a lecture at the University of Idaho on Ezra Pound. Earlier Dickey had tended to lump Pound with Eliot as a modernist who sought to give his readers not himself but *culture*. Dickey's revaluation is similar to the current revisionist view that sees Pound still as an influence on Eliot and on modernism but also as an influence on a much less impersonal and freer postmodernism. What he now finds valuable is not the "academic Pound of quotation and cultural cross-reference" but rather the Pound of "the amazing image," "the fresh clean language," and "the sound of a voice saying something simple and extraordinary" with the tone "of a delivered truth."[10] What Dickey finds of use in this Pound is not "the shock of recognition" but "the shock of possibility."

It is the tiny essay in the privately published *Billy Goat* that makes clear James Dickey's continuing commitment to his version of a Whitmanesque role for the poet, an intensified poet who establishes the necessary connections to make possible an intensified reader. There has been a slight change in terminology. He now desires an "energized man," nothing as sensational as a man "like a creature from another planet, giving off strange rays of solar energy," but simply "a human creature, like you, like me—like you *could be,* like I like to think I could be."[11]

The existential literature of three decades ago was once described as "the literature of possibility."[12] That phrase would be apt for a description of the kind of freedom that James Dickey desires for poets today, certainly for himself.

Chapter Nine
Afterword

Dickey has been too simply classified as being of the "more life" school of poetry. The description is partially true; but it implies a mindless romanticism, and it fails to distinguish Dickey's brand of neoromanticism from that of writers like the Beat poets, whom he detests and regards as advocating spontaneity and sensation as ends in themselves. Dickey may seem like them, but he is not *of* them. What he champions is a more intensified life, a more energized and more totally responsive man than modern urbanized life and the limitations inherent in specialization have permitted most men to be. At the same time, the formalist in Dickey is aware of the dangers of too much spontaneity, too much emotion, without the control imposed by grappling with form.

Dickey has also been regarded as writing in a social vacuum, or being a primitivist, an escapist, or a southern conservative insensitive to social problems. But Dickey's relationship to his society is not entirely negative or escapist. He desires as a poet the imaginative freedom to be apart from his society when he chooses but also the capacity to return to it, perhaps with an emotional or spiritual difference. He writes in *Sorties* that "there should be the capacity and elasticity in the mind of man to sit out on the side of a hill like a cave man, noting it all, being amazed by it all, and still be able to enter, perhaps with only a few scars, a technological environment, and see the possibilities—moral, aesthetic, and physical of that" (*S,* 29).

We have tried to make it clear that what Dickey has promoted in poetry and in prose is not a return to primitivism as better than civilized life but rather what he calls "emotional primitivism" and defines as that "condition where we can connect with whatever draws us" (*S,* 203). Man needs to regain the power that permits that condition again. Dickey desires to live the civilized life but also to retain the ability for primitive forces to "draw us." He reimagines for the poet who has become too tame and academic the ability to make connections with primordial life in order to

136

recapture for the personal consciousness whatever elements of the collective unconsciousness might be needed for both survival and joy. Some of the prophetic role of the poet should be restored. It is the poet who should be able to point the way "back even farther than the poetry of the tribe . . . back to the state of the first man himself, who stood on the shore and opened his arms to the world, that he and the world might possess each other" (*S,* 206). Dickey's poet can accomplish this through his imaginative ways of exchange and of making connections with "the other." Dickey is not, however, a latter-day D. H. Lawrence. He does not offer a program for regaining the cosmos, to find other selves than the ordinary, but he does provide the poetry and the prose to urge and to inspire his reader. Dickey as neoromantic is an advocate of vision and poetic obsession, even madness, but—no fool—he knows that they must be brought under control.

What we have argued is that Dickey, as poet and critic, retains the dual view characteristic of the modernist writer. For all his apparent neoromanticism, the formalist in Dickey counters with a poetry clearly something *made* but also the product of considerable imaginative freedom: "Language matters; technique matters; even God uses it" (*S,* 9). He makes it known that he wants to give his reader "a different version from the official version that God made or the World made us" (*S,* 9). He has his own way of reassociating the dissociated poet. He desires the poet in himself and in those he reads to use everything he has in order to write "complete poetry"—to help us realize all the potential selves unrealized within us and all the latent meanings within the actual world.

If Dickey has fostered subjectivity in poetry, it is because he has faith in "the protean qualities" of the artistic self. His poems either are personal or they seem personal, but like Proteus they are not limited to ordinary experiences or shapes. In his best poems Dickey has recaptured the excitement that he believes only a convincing persona, a thinking and feeling self in the poem, can convey. This strength has, however, become a source of criticism by those who believe that Dickey is good at what he does best but that he is limited in range and in subject. We have tried to show that his limitations have been exaggerated; his versatility, underrated. He can, for example, write the elegant declarative sentences of his early poetry and the sprawling, momentous lines of "Falling" and "May Day Sermon." His precisely balanced lyric impressions are matched by his compelling, direct narratives. And, with the vision of "country surrealism," he can step into stream-of-consciousness and hardly miss a stroke.

The questions about Dickey that his most recent poetry has not resolved are (1) whether, as literary persona, he can successfully distance himself from his own real life and still write poetry that makes the connections required for the reader, and (2) whether he can continue expanding his imaginings and his forms as much as he did during that first marvelous ten years, 1957–1967. In more recent poems, as in a few in *The Strength of Fields,* he seems to pull back and risk being ordinary, and being merely that is something the Dickey of magic eyes and sharp critique would be unable to tolerate for long.

Popular and critical interest in James Dickey has bent to the man as well as to the writer. He had contributed to the confusion of personae and self by telling so much about himself and about the origins of his poems in autobiographical experiences. When Dickey's poetic reputation was ascending, the stories about him were told with amusement as about a poet who was also a distinctive personality. Later, in the 1970s, when his poetic productivity waned and more reviewers became critical of his attempts to find new directions, amusement became disapproval, and much of the gossip turned nasty.

The trail of Dickey stories is long and intricate, with the recurrent themes of excess and outrage. Sometimes it is bizarre, and often, just plain sad. Much of the alcoholic and sexual legendry is apparently self-generated—as legendry frequently is—part of the showmanship of the ad-man-for-poetry role Dickey gladly accepted in the mid-1960s. Since the mid-1970s, however, the flood of new tales has abated somewhat. Perhaps it was the poet's own disclosures in *Self-Interviews* and *Sorties* about drinking and carousing in general; perhaps the public just grew bored with the spectacle. The abatement, nonetheless, is gratifying for those who have admired Dickey's work, and especially for those of us whose memories of the man include the gracefully intelligent, warm and playful conversations, the spontaneous acts of generosity, and the rare times of vulnerability that allow the public man to rest a while and the private peace to settle.

The death of his wife Maxine, the accumulation of his health problems, his marriage to Deborah and their concerted efforts against "giving alcohol another chance to let me know how good it is," all in the late 1970s, seem to be assimilating into a new creative phase in Dickey. He is keeping "four typewriters going all over the house now," Deborah has said, and the hopefulness is full, assisted by the birth of a daughter, Bronwen, in Dickey's fifty-eighth year. As of this writing, his projects abound in number and variety. Of specific note are his recent educational television appearances with Malcolm Muggeridge on the *Men of Letters* series; his study of Appalachia, *Wilderness of Heaven,* a second collaboration with artist Hubert Shuptrine; and the long-awaited novel, *Alnilam,* most recently called *A Minor Constellation.* And it certainly seems time, as Dickey enters his sixties, for a true "collected poems," which is anticipated.

Dickey has been too readily dismissed by many; the reassessment is due; the signs are here. More theses and dissertations emerge; more comprehensive essays appear in prestigious journals like *American Literature*; the blinding, prejudicial passions of the 1960s and 1970s have mellowed, as has Dickey himself. We have not pretended that Dickey has no faults, but even that distortion would have been more honorable than to pretend—as some have—that he has no virtues. A fair reading he deserves, for his achievement is great.

Notes and References

Chapter One

1. Yevgeny Yevtushenko, *Stolen Apples,* tr. James Dickey et al. (Garden City, N.Y.: Doubleday, 1971).
2. *Atlanta Constitution,* 18 February 1980, p. 18.
3. *Clemson Tiger,* 15 October 1942, carries an account of Dickey's exploits in the freshman game with South Carolina. Much of the material about Dickey at Clemson comes from conversations with former teachers and coaches during the time of Dickey's first poetry reading at Clemson, April 1966.
4. See Paul O'Neill, "The Unlikeliest Poet," *Life,* 22 July 1966, pp. 68–70, 72, 74, 77, 79.
5. Dickey's account is in *Self-Interviews* (Garden City, N.Y., 1971), p. 43. He experienced other incidents, even at Clemson in 1966, when his reading "The Sheep Child" led to a few protests to the Clemson University administration.
6. Richard Howard, *Alone with America* (New York.: Atheneum, 1980), p. 121.
7. R. P. Warren, "A Poem About the Ambition of Poetry," *New York Times Book Review,* 14 November 1976, p. 8.
8. Dave Smith, "The Strength of James Dickey," *Poetry* 137 (March 1981):355.

Chapter Two

1. John Hall Wheelock, ed., *Poets of Today VII* (New York: Scribner's, 1960), pp. 33–92.
2. Laurence Lieberman, "The Worldly Mystic," in *James Dickey: The Expansive Imagination,* ed. Richard J. Calhoun (Deland, Fla., 1973), pp. 65–76.
3. Wheelock, "Some Thoughts on Poetry," introduction to *Poets of Today,* pp. 13–32.
4. James Dickey, "The Energized Man," *Billy Goat 2* (Clemson, S.C.: Billy Goat Press, 1979), pp. 1–3.
5. Laurence Lieberman, *The Achievement of James Dickey* (Glenview, Ill., 1968), p. 8.
6. See William J. Martz, *The Distinctive Voice: Twentieth-Century American Poetry* (Glenview, Ill.: Scott, Foresman, 1966).

7. Randall Jarrell, *The Complete Poems* (New York: Farrar, Straus & Giroux, 1969), p. 144.

8. Michael Goldman, "Inventing the American Heart," *Nation,* 24 April 1967, p. 529.

9. Wheelock, *Poets of Today,* pp. 13–32.

10. Dickey, "The Energized Man," p. 2.

Chapter Three

1. Richard Howard, *Alone with America* (New York: Atheneum, 1980), p. 99.

2. Ibid., p. 102.

3. Ibid., p. 119.

4. Robert Langbaum, *The Modern Spirit: Essays on the Continuity of Nineteenth- and Twentieth-Century Literature* (New York: Oxford University Press, 1970), p. 19.

5. Joseph Conrad, *The Heart of Darkness,* ed. Robert Kimbrough (New York: W. W. Norton, 1963), p. 5.

6. Czeslaw Milosz, "Ars Poetica?" *Antaeus* 30/31 (Spring 1978):148–49.

Chapter Four

1. John Milton, "Lycidas," 1. 183; also observed by Ross Bennett, "The Self, the Imagination, and Survival in the Poetry of James Dickey," Ph.D. Diss., University of Newcastle (Australia), 1978, p. 46.

2. Wendell Berry, "James Dickey's New Book," *Poetry* 105 (November 1964):130–31.

3. Richard Howard, *Alone with America* (New York: Atheneum, 1980), p. 105.

4. Charles C. Tucker, "Major Themes in the Poetry of James Dickey," M.A. Thesis, North Texas State University, 1975, p. 92, n. 70.

5. Benjamin DeMott, "The 'More Life' School and James Dickey," *Saturday Review,* 28 March 1970, p. 38.

6. Ibid.

7. *Alone with America,* p. 113.

8. Robert Bly, "The Collapse of James Dickey," *Sixties* 9 (Spring 1967):70–79.

9. Howard, *Alone with America,* p. 112.

Chapter Five

1. In Calhoun, *James Dickey,* p. 177.

2. Laurence Lieberman, "Notes on James Dickey's Style," in Calhoun, *James Dickey,* p. 199.

3. Ibid., p. 185.

4. Jane Bowers Martin, "'With Eyes Far More Than Human': Transcendence in the Poetry of James Dickey," M.A. Thesis, Clemson University, 1978, p. 17.

5. Hill and Martin's discussion with Dickey, 30 October 1977, Columbia, S.C.

6. Martin, "'With Eyes,'" p. 6.

7. Ibid.

Chapter Six

1. Howard, *Alone with America,* p. 121.

2. Randall Jarrell, *The Complete Poems* (New York: Farrar, Straus & Giroux, 1969), p. 144.

3. Robert Penn Warren, "A Poem About the Ambition of Poetry," *New York Times Book Review,* 14 November 1976, p. 8.

4. Dave Smith, "The Strength of James Dickey," *Poetry* 137 (March 1981):352.

5. Hendrik Marsman, "The Zodiac," tr. A. J. Barnouw, *Sewanee Review* 55 (1947):238–51.

6. Smith, "The Strength of James Dickey," p. 352.

7. James Dickey, "Why I Live Where I Live," *Esquire,* April 1981, p. 63.

8. James Dickey, "Rootlight," *Gentleman's Quarterly* 48 (Winter 1978/79):146.

9. Smith, "The Strength of James Dickey," p. 352.

Chapter Seven

1. Franklin Ashley, "James Dickey: The Art of Poetry," *Paris Review* 65 (Spring 1976):54.

2. Bly, "The Collapse of James Dickey," pp. 70–79.

3. Anthony Thwaite, "Act of Bondage," *New Statesman,* 1 September 1970, pp. 310–13.

4. Benjamin DeMott, "The 'More Life' School and James Dickey," *Saturday Review,* 28 March 1970, p. 38.

5. Ashley, "James Dickey," p. 77.

6. David Arnett, "James Dickey: Poetry and Fiction," Ph.D. Diss., Tulane University, 1973, p. 192.

7. Ashley, "James Dickey," pp. 79–80.

8. Ibid., p. 80.

9. Peter Beidler, "'The Pride of Thine Heart Hath Deceived Thee': Narrative Distortion in Dickey's *Deliverance,*" *South Carolina Review* 5 (December 1972):20.

10. Jarrell, *Complete Poems,* p. 215.

11. Carolyn Kizer and James Boatwright, "A Conversation with James Dickey," *Shenandoah* 18 (Autumn 1966):3–28; reprinted in Calhoun, *James Dickey,* pp. 1–33.

12. DeMott, "The 'More Life' School," p. 23.

13. Arnett, "James Dickey," p. 209.

14. Cahill is Blind," *Esquire,* February 1976, pp. 67–69, 139–144.

15. David Morrison, "Wilderness of Heaven," *Atlanta Weekly,* 1 February 1981, pp. 10–17, 22–23.

Chapter Eight

1. Warren's comment is discussed in Franklin Ashley, "James Dickey: The Art of Poetry," *Paris Review* 65 (Spring 1976):70.

2. James Dickey, *Babel to Byzantium* (New York, 1968), p. ix. Dickey has frequently repeated this comment. Neither in writings nor in public readings does he refer to himself as a critic.

3. Ashley, "James Dickey," p. 81.

4. Ibid., p. 170.

5. Bly, "The Collapse of James Dickey," pp. 70–79.

6. Kizer and Boatwright, "A Conversation with James Dickey," pp. 3–28.

7. James Dickey, "The Greatest American Poet," *Atlantic Monthly,* November 1968, pp. 53–58.

8. James Dickey, "The Poet of Secret Lives and Misspent Opportunities," *New York Times Book Review,* 18 May 1969, pp. 1, 10.

9. James Dickey, "The Self as Agent," in *The Great Ideas Today,* ed. Robert M. Hutchins and Mortimer J. Adler (Chicago: Encyclopaedia Britannica, 1968), pp. 91–97; James Dickey, "The Son, the Cave, and the Burning Bush," in *The Young American Poets,* ed. Paul Carroll (Chicago: Follett; Big Table, 1968), pp. 7–19.

10. James Dickey, *The Water-Bug's Mittens: Ezra Pound: What We Can Use* (Bloomfield Hills, Mich.; Columbia, S.C.: Bruccoli Clark, 1980), p. 15.

11. James Dickey, *Billy Goat 2* (Clemson, S.C.: Billy Goat Press, 1979), p. 3.

12. See Hazel Barnes, *Humanistic Existentialism: The Literature of Possibility* (Lincoln: University of Nebraska Press, 1959).

Selected Bibliography

PRIMARY SOURCES

1. Poetry

Buckdancer's Choice. Middletown, Conn.: Wesleyan UP, 1965. (Cited as *BC.*)

Drowning with Others. Middletown, Conn.: Wesleyan UP, 1962. (Cited as *DWO.*)

Exchanges. Bloomfield Hills, Mich.: Bruccoli Clark, 1971.

The Eye-Beaters, Blood, Victory, Madness, Buckhead and Mercy. Garden City, N.Y.: Doubleday, 1970; London; Hamish Hamilton, 1971. (Cited as *EB.*)

Head-Deep in Strange Sounds. Winston-Salem, N.C.: Palaemon, 1979.

Helmets. Middletown, Conn.: Wesleyan University Press, 1964; London: Longmans, 1964. (Cited as *H.*)

Into the Stone and Other Poems. In *Poets of Today VII,* pp. 33–92. Edited by John Hall Wheelock. New York.: Scribner's, 1960. (Cited as *IS.*)

Poems (1967). Melbourne, Australia: Sun Books, 1968.

Poems 1957–1967. Middletown, Conn.: Wesleyan University Press, 1967; London: Rapp & Carroll, 1967. (Cited as *P.*)

Puella. Garden City, N.Y.: Doubleday, 1982.

The Strength of Fields. Garden City, N.Y.: Doubleday, 1979. (Cited as *SF.*)

Tucky the Hunter (juvenile). New York: Crown, 1978; London: Macmillan, 1979.

Two Poems of the Air. Calligraphy by Monica Moseley Pincus. Portland, Oreg.: Centicore Press, 1964.

The Zodiac. Garden City, N.Y.: Doubleday, 1976. (Cited as *Z.*)

2. Fiction

Deliverance. Boston: Houghton Mifflin, 1970; London: Hamish Hamilton, 1970. (Cited as *D.*)

3. Criticism and *Belles Lettres*

Babel to Byzantium: Poets & Poetry Now. New York: Farrar, Straus & Giroux, 1968. (Cited as *BB.*)

The Enemy from Eden. Northridge, Calif.: Lord John Press, 1978.
God's Images: The Bible, a New Vision. Etchings by Marvin Hayes. Birmingham,
    Ala.: Oxmoor House, 1977. (Cited as *GI.*)
In Pursuit of the Grey Soul. Columbia, S.C., and Bloomfield Hills, Mich.:
    Bruccoli Clark, 1978.
Jericho: The South Beheld. Paintings by Hubert Shuptrine. Birmingham, Ala.:
    Oxmoor House, 1974. (Cited as *J.*)
Metaphor as Pure Adventure. Washington, D.C.: Library of Congress, 1968.
A Private Brinksmanship. Claremont, Calif.: Pilzer College, 1965.
Self-Interviews. Edited by Barbara and James Reiss. Garden City, N.Y.: Double-
    day, 1971. (Cited as *SI.*)
Sorties: Journal and New Essays. Garden City, N.Y.: Doubleday, 1971. (Cited as
    S.)
Spinning the Crystal Ball. Washington, D.C.: Library of Congress, 1967.
The Suspect in Poetry. Madison, Minn.: Sixties Press, 1964. (Cited as *SP.*)
The Water-Bug's Mittens. Bloomfield Hills, Mich.: Bruccoli Clark, 1979.

4. Screenplays
Deliverance. Warner Brothers, 1972; Carbondale: Southern Illinois University
    Press, 1982.
Call of the Wild. Charles Fries, 1976.

5. Recordings
The Poems of James Dickey (1957–1967). Directed by Arthur Luce Klein. Spoken
    Arts (Sa 984) [LC No R67–39521]. New Rochelle, N.Y.: Spoken Arts,
    1967.

6. Films
A Poetry Experience on Film/Lord Let me Die/But Not Die Out/James Dickey: Poet.
    Chicago: Encyclopaedia Britannica, 1970.

7. Periodical Publications

Uncollected Poetry
"Purgation" [*homage, Po Chü-yi*]. *Kenyon Review,* n.s. 2 (Spring 1980):28–29.
"The Surround" [*James Wright Spoken-to at Sundown*]. *Atlantic Monthly,* July
    1980, p. 58.

Fiction
"Cahill Is Blind." *Esquire,* February 1976, pp. 67–69, 139–44.

Nonfiction
"Delights of the Edge." *Mademoiselle,* June 1974, pp. 118–19.

"Dialogues with Themselves." *New York Times Book Review,* 28 April 1963, p. 50.

"Excellently Bright, or Shell Roads." *Harper's Bazaar,* June 1981, pp. 81–82.

"The Geek of Poetry." Review of *Letters of Vachel Lindsay. New York Times Book Review,* 23 December 1979, pp. 9, 17–18.

"Look into Your Future Life Style." *Today's Health,* April 1973, pp. 54–55, 65 (truncated after p. 65).

"A Note on the Poetry of John Logan." *Sewanee Review* 70 (Spring 1962):257–60.

"An Old Family Custom." *New York Times Book Review,* 6 June 1965, pp. 1, 16.

"Reading." *Mademoiselle,* January 1973, pp. 133–34.

"Selling His Soul to the Devil by Day and Buying It Back by Night." *TV Guide,* 14 July 1979, pp. 18–20.

"The Triumph of Apollo 7." *Life,* 1 November 1968, p. 26.

"Why I Live Where I Live." *Esquire,* April 1981, pp. 63–64.

8. Interviews

Arnett, David L. "An Interview with James Dickey." *Contemporary Literature* 16 (Summer 1975): 286–300.

Ashley, Franklin. "The Art of Poetry XX: James Dickey." *Paris Review* 17 (Spring 1976):52–88.

Barnwell, W. C. "James Dickey on Yeats: An Interview." *Southern Review* 13 (Spring 1977):311–16.

Bruccoli, Matthew J. "James Dickey." In: *Conversations with Writers, 1,* pp. 25–45. Detroit: Bruccoli Clark/Gale Research, 1977.

Buckley, William F., Jr. *What Has Happened to the American Spirit?* Columbia, S.C.: Southern Educational Communications Association, 1971.

Cassidy, J. "Interview with James Dickey." *Writers Digest,* October 1974, pp. 16–24.

Davis, Will, et al. "James Dickey: An Interview." In: *James Dickey: Splintered Sunlight,* pp. 6–23. Edited by Patricia De La Fuente. Edinburg, Tex.: Pan American University, 1979.

Flake, Carol. "An Interview with James Dickey." *Baratraria Review* 1 (1974):5–11.

Graham, John. "James Dickey." In: *The Writer's Voice: Conversations with Contemporary Writers,* pp. 228–47. Edited by George Garrett. New York: Morrow, 1973.

Greiner, Donald J. " 'That Plain-Speaking Guy': A Conversation with James Dickey on Robert Frost." In: *Frost: Centennial Essays,* pp. 51–59. Edited by Jac L. Tharpe et al. Jackson: University Press of Mississippi, 1974.

Heyen, William. "A Conversation with James Dickey." *Southern Review* 9 (1973):135–56.

Kizer, Carolyn, and Boatwright, James. "A Conversation with James Dickey." *Shenandoah* 18 (Autumn 1966):3–28.

Moyers, Bill. *A Conversation with James Dickey.* New York: WNET/13, Educational Broadcasting Corp., 1976.

Packard, William, ed. *The Craft of Poetry: Interviews from "The New York Quarterly,"* pp. 133–51. Garden City, N.Y.: Doubleday, 1974.

SECONDARY SOURCES

1. Bibliographies

Ashley, Franklin. *James Dickey: A Checklist.* Columbia, S.C., and Detroit: Bruccoli Clark/ Gale Research, 1972. A list of all books and pamphlets by Dickey up to 1972 with photographs of their title pages. Still of value though sometimes inaccurate and largely superseded by Elledge.

Elledge, Jim. *James Dickey: A Bibliography, 1947–1974.* Metuchen, N.J., and London: Scarecrow, 1979. The most complete descriptive bibliography. An invaluable aid limited only by the fact that, though published in 1979, it includes items only through 1974.

Glancy, Eileen K. *James Dickey: The Critic as Poet: An Annotated Bibliography with an Introductory Essay.* Troy, N.Y.: Whiston, 1971.

2. Books, Pamphlets, and Dissertations

Arnett, David Leslie. "James Dickey: Poetry and Fiction." Ph.D. Diss., Tulane University, 1973. Valuable for the interview with Dickey on *Deliverance,* and its stress (though overstated) on what Arnett calls "the Epipsychidion theme" ("the birth of recognition of a superior soul . . . at specific moments in life") in Dickey's poetry.

Berry, David Chapman, Jr. "Orphic and Narcissistic Themes in the Poetry of James Dickey, 1951–1970." Ph.D. Diss., University of Tennessee, 1973. A study of Dickey's use of mythology. It is important for its detailed analysis of the Orphic motif in Dickey's poetry.

Calhoun, Richard J., ed. *James Dickey: The Expansive Imagination.* Deland, Fla.: Everett/Edwards, 1973. A collection of previously published essays with several new essays. This collection reprints some of the best essays on Dickey, such as those by Davison, Lieberman, and Weatherby (see under "Articles"), plus valuable new essays by George Lensing and Thomas O. Sloan. There is a selected bibliography by Robert W. Hill.

Lieberman, Laurence. *The Achievement of James Dickey: A Comprehensive Selection of His Poems with a Critical Introduction.* Glenview, Ill.: Scott, Foresman, 1968. Still a valuable discussion of Dickey themes—his concern with war, death, animals, family, death, with a special stress on joy/ celebration as a central quality of Dickey's poetic vision.

3. Articles and Parts of Books

Baughman, Ronald. "James Dickey's "The Eye-Beaters." *South Carolina Review*

10 (April 1978):81–88. One of the most detailed analyses of *The Eye-Beaters*. Attempts to find the emergence of a new poetic self in the poems in this volume and emphasizes the isolation of the self and estrangements rather than the earlier emphasis on union and exchange of identity.

Bennett, Ross. "'The Firebombing': A Reappraisal." *American Literature* 52 (November 1980):430–48. The most thorough explication of the poem. Analysis of thematic motifs and multiple point of view. Argues that this is a poem about self-discovery and perhaps one of the most important American poems since 1945.

Berry, David C. "Harmony with the Dead: James Dickey's Descent into the Underworld." *Southern Quarterly* 12 (April 1974):233–44. Develops the stress in Berry's dissertation on the Orphic theme in Dickey's poetry. Some parts of the Orphic myth, such as "The celebration of knowledge gained from the descent into Hades," are more relevant to Dickey's motifs than others.

Bly, Robert. "The Collapse of James Dickey." *Sixties* 9 (Spring 1967):70–79. The title appears only in the table of contents. A review of *Buckdancer's Choice* that accuses Dickey of a lack of social and political consciousness at a time when many poets, including Bly, were engaged in active protest against the war in Vietnam.

Calhoun, Richard J. "Whatever Happened to the Poet-Critic?" *Southern Literary Journal,* s. s. 1 (Autumn 1968):75–88. Stresses the importance of Dickey's program for returning subjectivity and personality to poetry in his opposition to impersonality and academicism. Wishes Dickey would write more literary criticism.

Carroll, Paul. "James Dickey's *Poems 1957–1967:* A Personal Appraisal." *Georgia Review* 22 (Spring 1968):12–23. An attempt to see Dickey's poetry over the ten-year period as expression of a unified view of poetry.

Davison, Peter. "The Difficulties of Being Major." *Atlantic Monthly,* October 1967, pp. 116–21. Regards Dickey and Lowell as major poets; compares and contrasts the two with stress on themes of war and reincarnation. (Reprinted in Calhoun, *James Dickey: The Expansive Imagination*—see above.)

Demott, Benjamin. "The 'More Life' School and James Dickey." *Saturday Review,* 28 March 1970, pp. 25–26, 38. View of Dickey as part of a neo-romantic movement that grasps for the absolute and dismisses the conventional modes of living.

Greiner, Donald J. "The Harmony of Bestiality in James Dickey's *Deliverance*." *South Carolina Review* 5 (December 1972):43–49. Important as a survey of critical impressions of *Deliverance*. Explains popularity of novel as due in part to its demonstration of presence of the savage beneath the veneer of civilization in all men.

Howard, Richard. "On James Dickey." *Partisan Review* 33 (Summer 1966):414–28, 479–86. Important discussion of symbols, images, and themes in Dickey's major poems. A positive attitude toward Dickey's poetry by a major critic. Detailed comparison and contrast of a large number of Dickey's poems.

Jameson, Frederic. "The Great American Hunter, or Ideological Content in the Novel." *College English* 34 (November 1972):180–97. Interesting as a neo-Marxist analysis of *Deliverance* by a leading authority on Marxist criticism.

Lensing, George. "The Neo-Romanticism of James Dickey." *South Carolina Review* 10 (April 1978):20–32. Valuable for detailing Dickey's challenge to doctrines of T. S. Eliot and for attempting to define Dickey's relationship to neo-romanticism of Theodore Roethke.

Lieberman, Laurence. "The Expansionist Poet: A Return to Personality." *Yale Review* 57 (December 1967):258–71. Important early recognition of the place of subjectivity in Dickey's poetry.

————. "The Worldly Mystic." *Hudson Review* 20 (Autumn 1967):513–20. Valuable for stress on dualisms in Dickey's poetry, materialism, and mysticism, the rational and irrational. (Reprinted in Calhoun—see above.)

Markos, Donald W. "Art and Immediacy: James Dickey's *Deliverance.*" *Southern Review,* n.s. 7 (July 1971):947–53. Interesting as a review which rebuts DeMott's "The 'More Life' School and James Dickey." Relates characters in the novel to Dickey's own character and to his literary motifs.

Mills, Ralph J., Jr. "The Poetry of James Dickey." *Triquarterly* 11 (Winter 1968):231–42. Important as a discussion of Dickey's themes, images, techniques. Ends with a negative view of the moral vision in Dickey's poetry.

Samuels, Charles Thomas. "What Hath Dickey Delivered?" *New Republic,* 18 April 1970, pp. 23–26. A good review of *Deliverance* that takes note of the epigrams, the relationship of the novel to the poem "On the Coosawattee," and the theme of homosexuality in the novel.

Silverstein, Norman. "James Dickey's Muscular Eschatology." *Salmagundi* 22–23 (Spring–Summer 1973):258–68. Perceptive view of Dickey's relationship to Southern Agrarians and the movement from poetry to an interest in prose.

Weatherby, H. L. "The Way of Exchange in James Dickey's Poetry." *Hudson Review* 74 (July–September 1966):669–80. Important essay for identifying and discussing Dickey's tendency in many of his major poems to exchange identity with the "other," often a primitive or frightening aspect of nature. (Reprinted in Calhoun—see above.)

Index